Abbreviations

ABF	Allah Bund Fault
ADC	Analog to Digital Convertor
ADMB	Aravalli Delhi Mobile Belt
AIN	Angle of Incidence
AK	Achankovil
AMD	Atomic Mineral Division
ANF	Alokananda Fault
ARL	Anjar Rapar Lineament
ASR	Andaman Spreading Ridge
BARC	Bhaba Atomic Research Centre
BARS	Belt of Active Rift Systems
BA	Burmese Arc
BB	Broad Band
BC	Bhandra Craton
BIS	Bureau Indian Standard
BN	Bundelkhund
BL	Bhachau Lineament
BS	Bastar Craton
BSF	Barwani Sukta Fault
BT	Basement Thrust
BTF	Basement Thrust Front
CBR	Carlsberg ridge
CCR	Central Core Region
CESS	Centre for Earth Science Studies
CGS	Coast and Geodetic Survey
CIS	Central India Suture
CMB	Core Mantle Boundary
CMP	Common Midpoint
CMT	Centroid Moment Tensor
CRB	Cambay Rift Basin
CRS	Central Recording Station
CSIR	Council of Scientific and Industrial Research
CWPRS	Central Water and Power Research Station
DAFB	Delhi Aravalli Fold Belt

Db.F	Dhubri Fault
DD	Double Difference
DF	Dauki Fault
DSS	Deep Seismic Soundings
DST	Department of Science and Technology
DVP	Deccan Volcanic Province
EDC	East Dharwar Craton
EGF	Empirical Green's Function
EGGB	Eastern Ghat Granulite Belt
EGMB	Eastern Ghat Mobile Belt
ER	East Ridge
ERI	Earthquake Research Institute (Japan)
ESC	European Seismological Commission
GBF	Great Boundary Fault
GDSN	Global Digital Seismic Network
GERI	Gujarat Engineering Research Institute
GL	Goalpara lineament
GMT	Greenwich Mean Time
GPS	Global Positioning System
GR	Godavari Rift
G-R	Gutenberg and Richter
GSHAP	Global Seismic Hazard Assessment Programme
GSI	Geological Survey of India
GSN	Global Seismographic Network
GTF	German Task Force
HFF	Himalayan Frontal Fault
HFT	Himalayan Frontal Thrust
HFU	Heat Flow Unit
HRV	Harvard University
HSB	Himalayan Seismic Belt
HVZ	High Velocity Zone
HYB	Hyderabad
IASPEI	International Association of Seismology and Physics of the Earth's Interior
IBF	Island Belt Fault
IGAP	Indo-Gangetic Alluvial Plains
IGP	Indo-Gangetic Plains
IIT (K)	Indian Institute of Technology (Kharagpur)
IIT(R)	Indian Institute of Technology (Roorkee)
ILTP	Integrated Long Term Program (Indo-Russian)
IMD	India Meteorological Department
INDEPH	International Deep Profiling in Tibet and Himalaya
IRIS	Incorporated Research Institute for Seismology
ISC	International Seismological Centre
ISPP	Indo Stanvac Petroleum Project
ISR	Institute of Seismological Research

IST	Indus Suture Thrust
J-B	Jeffreys-Bullen
J&K	Jammu & Kashmir
JHD	Joint Hypocentre Determination
KaF	Karakuram Fault
KC	Karnataka Craton
KLP	Kalpa
KMF	Kutch Mainland Fault
KRB	Kutch Rift Basin
KSEB	Kerala State Electricity Board
KSZ	Koyna Seismic Zone
LET	Local Earthquake Tomography
LP	Long Period
LTA	Long Term Average
LVZ	Low Velocity Zone
MBT	Main Boundary Thrust
MCS	Mercalli-Cancani-Sieberg
MCT	Main Central Thrust
MERI	Maharashtra Engineering Research Institute
MEQ	Micro Earthquake
MG	Mahanadi Graben
MHSB	Main Himalayan Seismic Belt
MIL	Milne
M-K	Malda Kishenganj
MKN	Makni
MKT	Main Karakuram Thrust
MM	Modified Mercalli
MMT	Main Mantle Thrust
Moho	Mohorovičić
M-S	Munger-Saharsa
MSK	Medvedev-Sponheuer-Karnik
MSR	Munger Saharsa Ridge
MT	Magnetotelluric
NCSN	Northern California Seismic Network
NEIC	National Earthquake Information Center
NEZ	North Escarpment Zone
NGRI	National Geophysical Research Institute
NIED	National Research Institute for Earth Science and Disaster Prevention
NKF	North Kathiwar Fault
NNF	Narmada North Fault
NPF	Nagar Parkar Fault
NRB	Narmada Rift Basin
NSF	Narmada South Fault
NSL	Narmada-Son Lineament
OBS	Ocean Bottom Seismograph

OIL	Oil India Limited
ONGC	Oil & Natural Gas Commission (now Corporation)
PGA	Peak Ground Acceleration
PF	Patna Fault
RF	Rossi Forel
RIS	Reservoir Induced Seismicity
RMS	Root Mean Square
RRL - J	Regional Research Laboratory - Jorhat
RSVP	Rajmahal-Sylhet Volcanic Province
RTS	Reservoir Triggered Seismicity
SC	Singhbhum Craton
SCB	Saurashtra Continental Block
SCR	Stable Continental Region
SCSI	Small Computer System Interface
SCSN	Southern California Seismic Network
SEPB	South East Platformal Block
SEZ	South Escarpment Zone
SGT	Southern Granulite Terrain
SIRT	Simultaneous Iterative Reconstruction Technique
SMA	Strong Motion Array
SOI	Survey of India
SONATA	Son-Narmada-Tapti Lineament
SP	Short Period
SPS	Samples Per Second
SRN	Srinagar
SRO	Seismic Research Observatories
STA	Short Term Average
STF	Source Time Function
SVD	Singular Value Decomposition
TAN	Tandon
THDC	Tehri Hydro Development Corporation
THF	Trans-Himadri Fault
TL	Tapti Lineament
UNESCO	United Nations Educational, Scientific and Cultural Organization
UPS	Uninterrupted Power Supply
USGS	United States Geological Survey
VBB	Very Broadband
VUW	Victoria University of Wellington
WAF	West Andaman Fault
WCF	West Coast Fault
WDC	West Dharwar Craton
WIHG	Wadia Institute of Himalayan Geology
WK	Wajrakarur
WSZ	Warna Seismic Zone
WWSSN	World Wide Seismograph Station Network

1

Introduction

Seismology is the study of generation, propagation and recording of *elastic waves* or *seismic waves* in the Earth (and other celestial bodies) and of the source, which produces them. The sources can be natural earthquakes or man-made sources of deformational energy that generate the seismic waves. Study of the seismic waves of the Earth provides the highest resolution of the internal Earth structure that no other geophysical method can provide. It is a branch of geophysics with the highest societal impact, both in assessing and reducing earthquake hazards, and in understanding *seismotectonics,* the structure and dynamic processes of the Earth.

1.1 CLASSIFICATION OF EARTHQUAKES AND FREQUENCY-MAGNITUDE RELATION

Seismologists had used the words like *small, medium* or *large* to describe an earthquake size. After introduction of the Richter magnitude-scale (Richter, 1935), the classification has been more definite. Hagiwara (1964) classified the earthquakes, according to magnitude, as follows:

Magnitude (M)	Classification
$M \geq 8$	Great earthquake
$7 \leq M < 8$	Major or Large earthquake
$5 \leq M < 7$	Moderate earthquake
$3 < M < 5$	Small earthquake
$1 \leq M < 3$	Microearthquake
$M < 1$	Ultra-microearthquake

All earthquakes of magnitude less than 3 are generally called *micro-earthquakes.* Gutenberg and Richter (1941) found that the frequency of earthquake occurrence is related to their magnitudes. The frequency-magnitude relation is given by: $\log_{10} N = a - b\text{M}$, where N = number of earthquakes of magnitude M or greater, a and b are constants. The parameter b is often referred to *b-slope* or *b-value.*

Many studies of earthquake statistics show that in the normal cases the value of *b* is approximately 1.0, which means that the number of earthquakes increases tenfold for each decrease of one magnitude unit. Thus, if an area produces one earthquake of magnitude 4 in a month, it would produce 10 earthquakes of magnitude 3, 100 earthquakes of magnitude 2 and 1000 earthquakes of magnitude 1 in one month. Therefore, smaller the magnitude of the earthquakes, greater the amount of seismic data one can record. Microearthquake networks are designed to take an advantage of the above frequency-magnitude relation. Table 1.1 illustrates the global observations of frequency of occurrence of earthquakes since 1900, and Table 1.2 illustrates the number of earthquakes located by the National Earthquake Information Center (NEIC), US Geological Survey (USGS) for the period 1990-2002 and the estimated loss of lives.

Table 1.1: Frequency of occurrence of earthquakes based on observations since 1990, NEIC, USGS

Description	*Magnitude*	*Average Annually*
Great	8 and higher	1
Major	7 - 7.9	18
Strong	6 - 6.9	120
Moderate	5 - 5.9	800
Small	4 - 4.9	6,200 (estimated)
Minor	3 - 3.9	49,000 (estimated)
Microearthquakes	<3.0	Magnitude 2 – 3: about 1000 per day Magnitude 1 – 2: about 8000 per day

(Note: Description or classification as per USGS)

Table 1.2: Number of earthquakes worldwide, 1990-2000, NEIC, USGS

Magnitude	*1990*	*1991*	*1992*	*1993*	*1994*	*1995*	*1996*	*1997*	*1998*	*1999*	*2000*	*2001*	*2002*
8.0 to 9.9	0	0	0	1	2	3	1	0	2	4	1	1	0
7.0 to 7.9	12	11	23	15	13	22	21	20	14	23	14	15	13
6.0 to 6.9	115	105	104	141	161	185	160	125	113	113	158	126	133
5.0 to 5.9	1635	1469	1541	1449	1542	1327	1223	1118	979	982	1345	1243	1037
4.0 to 4.9	4493	4372	5196	5034	4544	8140	8794	7938	7303	6998	8045	8084	9034
Estimated Deaths	51916	2326	3814	10036	1038	7949	419	2097	8928	22711	231	21357	1711

1.2 HISTORICAL DEVELOPMENT OF EARTHQUAKE SEISMOLOGY AND GLOBAL NETWORK

Seismology is relatively a young science, which is basically developed with the evolution of theory of elasticity and development of instrumental and observational data base. Although the Chinese had a first operational seismic-wave detector (seismoscope) around 132 AD, the theoretical seismology was considerably ahead of observational seismology until late 1800s. The evolution came with the Hook's law indicating proportionality between stress and strain, which was followed by equations of elasticity by Navier and Canchy in 1921-22. In 1830, Poisson used the equations of motion and laws of elasticity to show two fundamental types of waves propagate through the interior of homogeneous solids. These two waves are *P wave* (Primary or Compressional wave) and *S wave* (Secondary or Shear wave). In 1887, Lord Rayleigh discovered existence of surface wave called *Rayleigh wave*, and in 1911 a second type of surface wave was discovered by A.E. Love, called *Love wave*. Both these waves are the results from the interaction of P and S waves with boundary conditions on the body with no shear stress of the surface.

International efforts led to the invention of the first *seismometer* by Filippo Cecchi in Italy in 1875 (Lay and Wallace, 1995). The sensitivity of early seismometer improved rapidly, and in 1889 accurate recording of seismic waves from a distant earthquake was possible in Potsdam, 15 minutes after the earthquake in Japan, demonstrating that the Earth behaves as a nearly elastic body in the frequency band of most seismic observations.

In early 1960s, a World Wide Seismograph Station Network (WWSSN) was established with identical sets of short-period and long-period three-component seismographs. This global network was equipped with very accurate timing by crystal clocks and standardized instrumentation; about 120 stations were in operation. The impact of the WWSSN was tremendous, coming at the time of *plate tectonics* revolution, when accurate seismic recordings and earthquake location were critical. In around 1975, the WWSSN was superseded by the Seismic Research Observatories (SRO), and eventually the network was digitally upgraded to the Global Digital Seismic Network (GDSN) in 1980s jointly by the Incorporated Research Institute for Seismology (IRIS) and the US Geological Survey (USGS). Due to large ocean surface as well as political situations, the network was not well distributed. The network is, however, growing continuously in collaboration with the French project GEOSCOPE together with instruments deployed by Australia, Canada, Europe and Japan. The ocean basins, of course, cause substantial gaps in the coverage, and Ocean Bottom Seismographs (OBS) are planned to minimize these gaps. In mid 2004, the Global Seismographic Network (GSN) surpasses its design goal (Park et al., 2005); a total of 136 GSN stations are now in operation from south pole to Siberia, and from Andaman basin to the sea floor of the northeast Pacific ocean. All GSN broadband data are freely available through the internet (www.iris.edu).

1.3 HISTORICAL DEVELOPMENT OF MICROEARTHQUAKE NETWORK

In terms of historical development, microearthquake networks evolved from temporary expeditions for aftershock study of large earthquakes to reconnaissance surveys, and finally mobile arrays to permanent telemetered networks. By the discovery of the earthquake frequency-magnitude relation (Gutenberg and Richter, 1941), methods and techniques to study microearthquakes have been developed by various groups of seismologist in several countries, like Japan, South Africa, USA and USSR. Although implementation of technological advances in instrumentation, data transmission and data processing in microearthquake networks was made in 1970s, many pioneering investigations were carried out in many countries much early. A detailed account of historical development is given by Lee and Stewart (1981). A brief outline is given here.

Japanese seismologists first developed portable and sensitive seismographs to study aftershocks, and Asada (1957) first reported a detailed study of microearthquakes. In the 1960s many microearthquake networks were established in Japan. These networks consisted 5-15 stations each and were reported by many groups (e.g. Suzuki et al., 1979).

In USA, the first microearthquake study was reported by Sanford and Holmes (1962) in a manner similar to Asada (1957). J.P. Eaton first developed a telemetered network for precise location of microearthquakes in Hawaii (Eaton, 1962). Since then several groups in the United States began microearthquake surveys, notable among them were J. Oliver and his group (e.g. Oliver et al., 1966), J.N. Brune and his group (e.g. Brune and Allen, 1967). A detailed study of the aftershocks of the 1966 Parkfield earthquake by Eaton et al. (1970a) demonstrated the usefulness of microearthquake networks in understanding the earthquake generating process, and made a great impact to develop the Central California Telemetric Network on large scale (Eaton et al., 1970b).

In India, microearthquake investigation started in 1978 for geothermal exploration in Puga valley and also to cater the need of river valley projects in 1980s in northwestern Himalaya (IMD, 1980 and 1988). K.N. Khattri and his group in the University of Roorkee (now Indian Institute of Technology, Roorkee), and S.N. Saha and his group in the Geological Survey of India (GSI) made a collaborative microearthquake investigation in northeast India region in 1980s (Khattri et al., 1983). The investigation in northeast India was extended by the author and his group in the GSI (e.g. Kayal, 1987; Kayal and De, 1987). Two permanent telemetric networks were established in late 1980s on experimental basis, one by the then University of Roorkee in Garhwal Himalaya, and the other by the NGRI in northeast India. The aftershock study of the 1991 Uttarkashi earthquake in the Garhwal Himalaya, and the aftershock study of the 1993 Killari (Latur) earthquake in Maharashtra, in particular, made tremendous impact on modernisation of the permanent seismological observatories as well as microearthquake networks in India. A great deal of effort has been made by the Department of Science and Technology (DST) to upgrade the permanent seismological observatories of the India Meteorological Department (IMD) to GSN standard, and to establish more permanent observatories and telemetric networks in different earthquake prone zones of the country. Many institutes and universities in the country are also funded by the DST for running microearthquake networks and permanent observatories.

1.4 APPLICATIONS OF MICROEARTHQUAKE NETWORK

Microearthquake networks are powerful tool for detailed seismological investigations. These networks generate large quantity of seismic data because of high occurrence-rate of microearthquakes. Applications of microearthquake networks are numerous; to name a few:

(i) mapping seismicity and active faults/lineaments,
(ii) studying focal mechanism of earthquakes, tectonic stress etc.,
(iii) investigating velocity structure of the crust and upper mantle,
(iv) exploring geothermal resources,
(v) investigating aftershocks, swarm activity etc.,
(vi) developing mining industry, hydel-dam projects, nuclear power plants etc.,
(vii) investigating Reservoir Induced Seismicity (RIS) and other man-made induced seismicity,
(viii) monitoring volcanic seismicity,
(ix) monitoring earthquake precursors, etc.

Results from these studies are integrated with other geophysical and geological field investigations for better understanding of earthquake processes, seismicity, seismotectonics, crustal structure, precursors etc. in South Asia region. A large quantity of local microearthquake and regional earthquake data are analysed to understand seismotectonics of the Himalaya from the westerm syntaxis, Pamir-Hindu Kush to eastern syntaxis, Arunachal Himalaya, and a 2500 km long Himalayan seismic belt. The seismic activity in the northeast India region as well as the intense activity along the Indo-Burma and Andaman-Sumatra arcs are well studied using the recent digital seismic network data at the atypical continental subduction zone beneath the Indo-Burma ranges and at the typical oceanic plate (Indian Ocean) subduction beneath the Andaman-Sumatra arc. The complex intraplate tectonics of peninsular India, Bangladesh and Sri Lanka are also well studied; the typical intraplate seismicity, RIS, aftershocks, swarms and active faults are investigated using the microearthquake network data.

2

Earthquakes and Seismic Waves

EARTHQUAKES

Earthquakes are exciting and sometimes devastating. A large earthquake attracts general attention because it causes damage to houses and other works of man, or breaks up and changes the ground surfaces. To the engineers, the earthquakes of great interest are those which affect the stability and safety of the buildings and other constructions. To the geologists, the earthquake phenomena of interest are the evidence of faulting or other tectonic process and the relation of earthquakes to the geological structures. And for the geophysicists or seismologists, every earthquake, large or small, presents a problem of explanation and interpretation of every wriggle of the seismic waves produced by the earthquakes. Earthquake seismology is thus defined to be a dual science, a border line field between geology and geophysics. It calls for sound physical and mathematical thinking, and a strong background of geological concepts.

2.1 TYPES OR CAUSES OF EARTHQUAKES

Earthquakes can be divided into four categories based on their mode of generation. These are discussed below:

2.1.1 Tectonic Earthquakes

Tectonic earthquakes are by far the most common earthquakes. These earthquakes are produced when the rocks fracture by various geological forces because of constant geological reshaping of the Earth. Tectonic earthquakes are most important to study the structure and interior of the Earth, and they are of much social significance as they pose greatest hazard.

Some earthquakes are, however, as deep as 700 km in some of the subduction zones, e.g. the Tonga Islands, Java Islands, the New Hebrides etc. Earthquakes, generally, with foci between 70-300 km deep are called *intermediate focus* and those below this depth are called *deep focus*. Along with the deep focus earthquakes, the chemical composition of rocks in the subducting plate changes. The molten fraction of rocks may be stored for a time in *magma chambers,* which are huge reservoirs underneath volcanic vents. From these pressure chambers magma moves upwards from time to time as lava. Thus, a volcanic arc is a typical characteristic in a subduction zone (Fig. 2.2). Further, interaction between the two plates, overriding continental plate and the subducting oceanic plate, near the trench causes folding, faulting and thrusting in the continental crust, and makes an exposure of ophiolite (oceanic crust) at the surface.

Collision Zone Earthquakes

Tectonic earthquakes are also produced at the edges of the interacting plates where the plates collide head on, and rise as mountain chains, e.g. the Himalayan belt in Indo-Eurasian collision zone, the Alpine belt in the eastern Europe, the Zagros thrust system in Iran (Fig. 2.1). The interplate earthquakes in collision zones are usually shallow (<100 km), and dominated by low angle thrusting, which is a manifestation of lithospheric shortening. These low angle faults/thrusts can generate large earthquakes as we see in the Himalayan belt.

Divergent and Transcurrent Plate Boundary Earthquakes

In general, divergent and transcurrent plate boundaries are characterized by much shallower seismicity (focal depth less than 30 km). The mid-oceanic ridges, the divergent zones, are the manifestation of shallow extensional faulting (Fig. 2.3). One of the interesting features of mid oceanic ridges is that they are offset by lineament known as fracture zones. Wilson (1965) proposed the concept of *transform faults* or *strike-slip faults* that accommodate ridge spreading. *Continental strike-slip* or *transcurrent plate boundary* may also be observed in continent-continent or oceanic-continental situation (Fig. 2.3). The most famous example in oceanic-continental situation is the San Andreas fault in California, which separates the North America and Pacific plates. Transcurrent plate boundary in continental settings is extremely important from seismic hazard point of view. A few examples of such continental transcurrent faults are the Anatolian fault in Turkey, Alpine fault in New Zealand and the Sagaing fault in Burma (Fig. 2.3). These transcurrent-fault earthquakes are shallow and sometimes produce large fatal earthquakes, e.g. the 1989 Loma Prieta earthquake on the San Andreas fault (Catchings and Kohler, 1996).

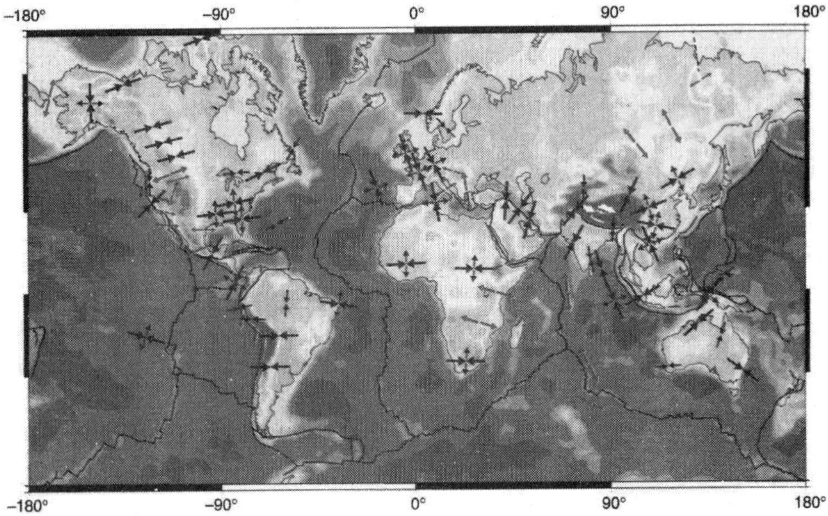

Fig. 2.3 World stress map (Zoback, 1992); inward pointed arrows indicate compression (thrust faulting), outward arrows tension (normal and strike slip faulting).

Intraplate Earthquakes

About 60 percent of the world's seismicity is mapped by the *interplate earthquakes* at the plate boundaries as stated above, and about 10 percent is mapped at the *spreading zones.* The world's seismicity map, however, shows that earthquakes do take place within the plate, far from the plate boundaries as well (Fig. 2.1). These earthquakes are called *intraplate earthquakes,* and they arise from the localised system of forces. The intraplate and interplate earthquakes differ in two important ways. First, the recurrence interval of intraplate earthquakes is generally much longer than those of the interplate earthquakes, and second, the intraplate earthquakes typically have much higher stress drops. Three large/fatal intraplate earthquakes (M 6.0~7.7) that have occurred in peninsular India during the last decade are discussed in Chapter 7.

Hypocentres of the earthquakes in the intraplate zones rarely occur deeper than 15-20 km. Deepest earthquakes indicate the base of the seismogenic zone, or bottom of the fault. Within the seismogenic zone the crust deforms either by stable or unstable sliding on the existing fault(s), or as a brittle material that fails generating a new fault, when subjected to stresses greater than the strength of the material. The strength depends on both temperature and pressure. The strength increases to a depth of about 15-20 km, and then decreases rapidly. Below the seismogenic zone stable sliding or ductile deformation takes place.

2.1.2 Volcanic Earthquakes

Volcanic earthquakes are defined as the earthquakes which occur or are linked up with the volcanic activity. These earthquakes occur in two ways.

First, often before an eruption minor seismic activity increases in the vicinity of the volcano. Some kilometres below the volcanic vent, very hot viscous magma moves sluggishly under high steam pressure through a network of veins and arteries from one storage chamber to another. Due to this motion, various parts of the surrounding rock become hotter and more strained as the magma pushes them. These forces fracture the neighbouring rocks, and the strain is relieved by small or moderate earthquakes. Second, sometimes fault rupture precedes the motion of magma and eruption of lava. The earthquake waves from the rupturing fault may shake up the molten material in the storage reservoir beneath the volcano. In a way, similar to the violent shaking of a bottle of soda pop, steam and gas that have previously dissolved in the magma begin to boil off and accelerate the escape of lava and gaseous material. This, in turn, would disturb the unstable equilibrium of the magma below the vent, and stimulate local volcanic earthquakes.

2.1.3 Induced Earthquakes

Some earthquakes are induced; this means that human activity triggers the earthquakes. These are: (i) *Reservoir Induced Seismicity* (RIS), (ii) *Nuclear explosion,* (iii) *Rock burst, fluid injection,* etc.

Reservoir Induced Seismicity

Reservoir induced earthquakes have been reported in conjunction with the impoundment of water or rapid water level changes behind large dams (Gupta and Rastogi, 1976). Since these earthquakes are triggered along pre-existing and pre-stressed tectonic faults, they show typical characteristics of *double couple sources* (see Section 4.6.1).

The December 10, 1967 Koyna earthquake (M 6.7) in India that caused a loss of about 200 human lives, is attributed to RIS for the Koyna dam (Gupta and Rastogi, 1976). It is unlikely that simply weight of the water, which would only add a tiny fraction of the total stress at a depth 3 or 5 km below the surface, causes the RIS. A more likely explanation is that the *pore pressure* increases because of the hydrostatic head of the reservoir. The RIS was first observed with the filling of Lake Mead behind Hoover Dam beginning in 1935 (Simpson, 1976). Before the reservoir was filled, the background seismicity was low; the seismicity began to rise in 1936, with occurrence of an earthquake M 5.0 in 1940. RIS is mostly shallow focus, less than 6 km. Damaging earthquakes M>6.0, that are referred to the RIS, occurred at Hsinfeugkiang, China in 1962, at Kariba, Zambia-Zimbabwe border in 1963, at Kremasta, Greece in 1966 and at Koyna, India in 1967 (Gupta, 1992). In a recent book on Reservoir Induced Earthquakes by Gupta (1992) all the necessary information on RIS has been given. In his recent review Gupta (2002), however, preferred the term RTS (Reservoir Triggered Seismicity) rather than the RIS.

Nuclear Explosion

The other man-made earthquake is the *nuclear explosion*. Theoretically the seismic waves generated by an underground nuclear explosion should be very different from shear motion that characterizes double-couple sources for natural earthquake. The nuclear explosion produces outward directed compressional motions in all directions while tectonic earthquake produces motions of different amplitude and polarity in different directions (see Section 4.6.2). So, the seismograms from an explosion should not have S_H or *Love waves*, but many explosions do have S_H type energy. This energy is thought to be the release of pre-existing strain by the explosion. A very good case study of the Indian nuclear explosion at the Pokhran-test site, Rajasthan on May 11, 1998, was made by Sikka et al. (1998). The estimated magnitude of this explosion was m_b = 5.4. They did not report S_H wave.

Rock Burst, Fluid Injection etc.

The third type of induced earthquakes are generated by rock burst, fluid or stream injection etc. Collapsing of the roof of mines and caverns, the so-called phenomena of *rock-burst*, occurs due to induced stress around the mine workings, and it produces seismic waves. Readers are referred to a review book on Mining Seismology by Gibowicz and Kijko (1994) for detailed information. Similarly, fluid or steam injection process in the oil fields for secondary production also causes minor tremors (e.g. Talebi and Cornet, 1987; Talebi et al., 1998). In a recent book, Guha (2000) has given a detailed review of induced seismicity.

2.2 TELESEISMIC, REGIONAL AND LOCAL EARTHQUAKES

Earthquakes may be further classified into three types depending on the distance from source to the *seismograph* station. Since the character of *seismograms* depends on *epicentral* distance, the nomenclature for seismic phases is also distant dependent.

2.2.1 Teleseismic Earthquakes

The earthquakes, which are recorded by a seismograph station at a greater distance, are called *teleseismic earthquakes*. These are very often called *teleseisms*. By international convention the epicentral distance is required to be more than 1000 km for a teleseism. Lay and Wallace (1995), however, define teleseismic distance as $\Delta \geq 30°$. An example of a tele-seismogram is shown in Fig. 2.4. Depending on the magnitude of the earthquake, teleseismic amplitudes can range from barely perceptible to those that saturate the instrument. These earthquakes provide very useful seismic phases for the crust as well as for the interior of the Earth. The direct P and S-wave arrivals recorded at teleseismic distances between 30° and 95° are relatively simple

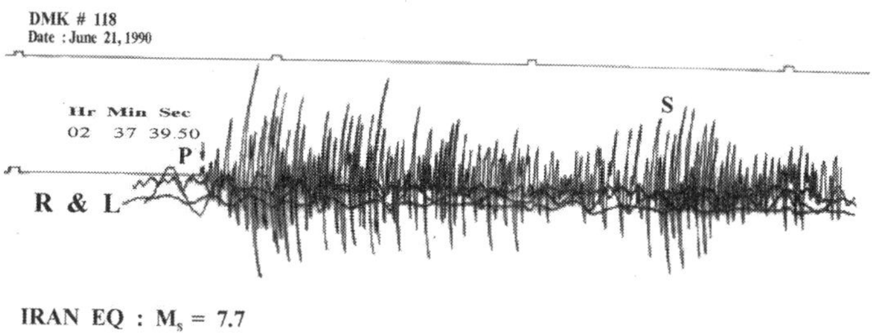

Fig. 2.4 Part of a tele-seismogram showing seismic phases of the Iran earthquake of June 21, 1990, Ms 7.7, recorded by a microearthquake recorder (PS-2) at a temporary seismograph station at DMK (Doimukh), Arunachal Pradesh, northeast India during a microearthquake survey. Minute marks are indicated by square pulses above. The seismic phases continued for more than 40 minutes. Long period surface waves (R & L) are also recorded (Kayal et al., 1993).

indicating a smooth velocity distribution. Beyond 95°, the direct phases become complicated due to interaction with the Earth's core (see Section 2.17).

2.2.2 Regional Earthquakes

The earthquakes, which occur beyond say 500 km but within 1000 km of a seismograph station, are called *regional earthquakes*. An example of a regional earthquake, recorded by a microearthquake recorder at a distance of about 700 km, is shown in Fig. 2.5. Like teleseismic events, amplitudes of regional

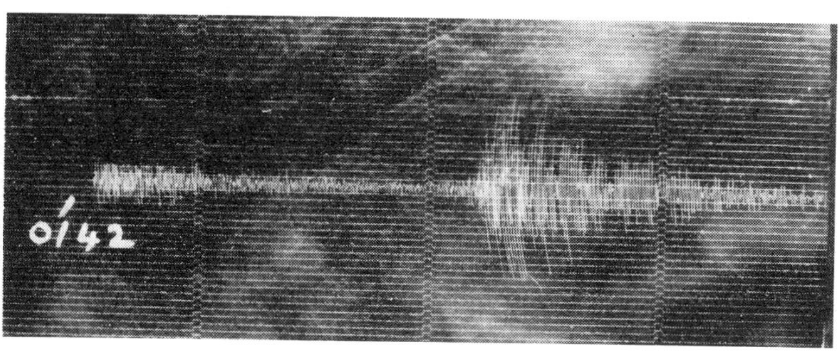

Fig. 2.5 Part of an original seismogram showing a regional earthquake recorded by a microearthquake recorder (PS-2) in northeast India region. The event is annotated by hr. min. (0142). The square pulses indicate the minute marks. The S-P interval is more than one minute (Kayal et al., 1993).

earthquakes can range from barely perceptible to large, but their periods are less than those of the teleseism. These earthquakes also provide seismic-wave data for the Earth's crust and mantle.

2.2.3 Local Earthquakes

Earthquakes occurring within a distance of few hundred km, say 500 km, from a seismic station are called *local earthquakes*. Local earthquakes are often characterised by impulsive onsets and high frequencies. A seismogram showing local earthquakes recorded by a microearthquake station at a distance ranging from 50 to 250 km is illustrated in Fig. 2.6. The local earthquake signal has typically an exponential decreasing tail. The seismic-wave data are very useful to study the local geological structure/velocity structure of the Earth's crust and upper mantle.

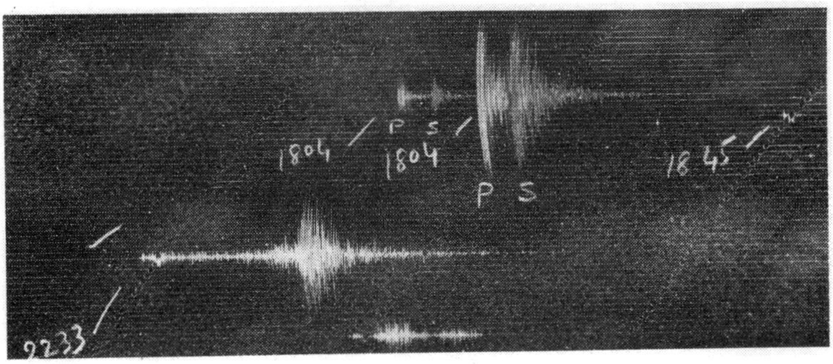

Fig. 2.6 Part of an original seismogram showing local earthquakes including microearthquakes; P and S phases are indicated. The S-P intervals are few seconds to less than a minute (Kayal, 1983). Other explanations are same as Fig. 2.5.

2.3 FORESHOCKS, AFTERSHOCKS AND EARTHQUAKE SWARMS

An earthquake of consequence is never an isolated event. A larger shock is likely to be preceded by a few smaller shocks; these are called *foreshocks*. There are, almost certain, to be many shocks after a main shock, which are called *aftershocks*. The aftershocks gradually decrease in frequency and magnitude. The foreshocks and aftershocks are expected to occur in the same epicentre area, and are, generally, associated with the same fault system of the main shock. On the other hand, a long series of small shocks with no main event is frequently recorded in certain localities; these sequences are called *earthquake swarms*.

2.3.1 Foreshocks

Evidence of *foreshocks* is hard to judge before the occurrence of a main event since there is nothing to distinguish foreshocks from the ordinary

small shocks in an active region. Suspicious series of small earthquakes may be followed by no main shock or by a sizable earthquake. Of earthquakes with M>7.0, about 70% are preceded by foreshocks. The nature of foreshock activity varies greatly, but it typically begins 5-10 days before the main shock.

Oldham (1899) reported no foreshock for the 1897 great Shillong earthquake (M 8.7); neither were any reported for the 1934 great Bihar-Nepal earthquake (M 8.4), nor for the 1950 great Assam-Tibet earthquake (M 8.7). By contrast, 1915 Nevada (USA) earthquake was preceded by many small foreshocks. Foreshocks subsequently are reported for many large earthquakes at various parts of the world and are used for earthquake precursor study. Jones and Molnar (1979) summarized the characteristics of foreshocks associated with major earthquakes of the world.

2.3.2 Aftershocks

Aftershocks are almost always reported after a sizable earthquake. The number, magnitude and the duration of aftershock activity depend on the size of main shock, depth and tectonic setting of the area. The aftershocks are apparently related to the fault plane that slipped during the main event. Båth (1979) noted that in many instances the largest aftershock is about 1.2 less in magnitude than that of the main shock. Aftershocks are more often journalistically called settling shocks, that is readjustment to equilibrium. Internal readjustment may be expected to go on for some time with decreasing frequency and magnitude of the aftershocks.

Aftershock Decay: Omori law

The decay of aftershock event rate $N(t)$ with time t was initially found to obey a simple hyperbolic law known as Omori law (Omori, 1894). More generally, Utsu (1957) showed that the rate of aftershock decay could be described by power law as:

$$N(t) \propto t^{-p} \qquad (2.1)$$

where p is the attenuation factor or rate, constant of aftershock decay. The eq (2.1) is called modified Omori formula (Utsu, 1957). Thus, the Omori law is equivalent to modified Omori formula with exponent $p = 1$. Several researchers have empirically shown that the p-values of large earthquakes are close to 1.0, but it ranges from 0.6 to 2.5 (e.g. Mogi, 1962; Utsu, 1969; Kisslinger and Jones, 1991; Guo and Ogata, 1995, 1997).

Aftershocks of second order may be closely followed by a trail of small shocks which fall off more rapidly than the general aftershock activity. Occurrence of second order aftershocks is explained by a larger aftershock event, which dynamically may be an independent earthquake.

Fault Area

The distribution of aftershocks is often used to infer the fault area of the main shock. For most earthquakes, the fault area or aftershock area scales with magnitude. Utsu and Seki (1954) developed an empirical formula:

$$\log A = 1.02\ M_S + 6.0 \tag{2.2}$$

where A is measured in cm^2, and M_S is surface wave magnitude of the earthquake (see Section 2.4). In general, the fault area is estimated from the extent of aftershock zone, one or two days after the main shock. This limit is imposed because sometimes aftershock zones grow continually for a month or more, presumably involving outward expansion of the main shock rupture zone (Lay and Wallace, 1995). The total seismic moment release by an aftershock sequence rarely exceeds 10% of the moment of the main shock.

As mentioned in Chapter 1, aftershock studies have greatly stimulated the development of microearthquake network. Vast quantities of data are recorded by deploying temporary seismograph stations for detailed studies of damaging earthquakes. Investigations of aftershocks for the recent damaging earthquakes during the last decade in India are discussed in Chapters 5–7.

2.3.3 Earthquake Swarms

Swarms are sequence of earthquakes that are clustered in space and time, and are not associated with identifiable main shock. The *b*-value for a swarm can be as high as 2.5, which implies that no large earthquake accompanies the occurrence of huge small magnitude earthquakes. The high *b*-value may be explained by weak crust, incapable of sustaining high strain levels and heterogeneous stress system in the shallow crust.

Earthquake swarms are common in volcanic regions, they occur before and during the eruptions. Swarms are also observed in non-volcanic areas, as in Comrie in Scotland and in the Vogtland on the southern border of Germany (Lee and Stewart, 1981) and in New Zealand (Kayal, 1983). Swarm activities in the Himalaya and in central India are also reported (see Chapters 5 and 7). Swarms of special pattern in time and space may indicate a precursory signal to an impending large earthquake (Evison, 1982). Earthquake swarm used as a precursor tool in forecasting a large Indo-Burma border earthquake is discussed in Chapter 6.

2.4 EARTHQUAKE MAGNITUDE, INTENSITY AND ENERGY

Magnitude is one of the basic and important parameters of an earthquake. It defines the size of an earthquake. The common people are, in general, confused about different scales of magnitude, and sometimes they mix-up earthquake intensity with its magnitude. Journalists often report the magnitude value of an earthquake as its intensity; this is wrong.

Intensity of an earthquake is a measure of its effect, i.e. degree of damage; for example broken windows, collapsed houses etc. produced by an earthquake at a particular place. The effect of the earthquake may cause collapsed houses at city A, broken windows at city B and no damage at city C. Intensity observations are, thus, subject to personal estimates and are limited by the circumstances of reported effects (Bolt, 1999). Intensity varies from place to place for the same earthquake. Therefore, it is desirable to have a scale for rating earthquakes in terms of energy, independent of the effects produced at a particular area. In response to this practical need, Richter (1935) first proposed a magnitude scale based solely on amplitudes of ground motion recorded by a seismograph.

2.4.1 Earthquake Magnitude

There are now different magnitude scales to define the size of an earthquake. After Richter (1935), various magnitude scales are proposed. The Richter scale and the recent theoretical based scales are discussed below.

Richter Magnitude (or Local Magnitude) M_L

Richter (1935) defined the local magnitude M_L of an earthquake observed at a station to be

$$M_L = \log A - \log Ao\ (\Delta) \tag{2.3}$$

where A is the maximum amplitude in millimetres recorded on the *Wood-Anderson seismograph* for an earthquake at epicentral distance of Δ km, and Ao (Δ) is the maximum amplitude at Δ km for a standard earthquake. The local magnitude is thus a number characteristic of the earthquake, and independent of the location of the recording station.

Three arbitrary choices are made in the above definition: (i) the use of standard Wood-Anderson seismograph, (ii) the use of common logarithms to the base 10, and (iii) selection of the standard earthquake whose amplitudes as a function of distance are represented by Ao (Δ). The zero level of Ao (Δ) can be fixed by choosing its value at a particular distance. Richter chose the zero level of Ao (Δ) to be 1 μm (or 0.001 mm) at a distance of 100 km from the earthquake epicentre. Thus, an earthquake with trace amplitude A = 1 mm recorded on a standard Wood-Anderson seismograph at a distance of 100 km is assigned magnitude 3. Richter arbitrarily chose –log Ao = 3 at Δ = 100 km so that the earthquakes do not have negative magnitudes. In other words, to compute M_L a table of –log Ao as a function of epicentral distance in kilometres is needed. Based on observed amplitudes of a series of well located earthquakes the table of –log Ao as a function of epicentral distance is given by Richter (1958).

In practice, we need to know the approximate epicentral distance of an earthquake, which can be estimated from S-P time. The maximum trace amplitude on a standard Wood-Anderson seismogram is then measured in millimetres, and its logarithm to base 10 is taken. This number is then added to the quantity tabulated as –log Ao for the corresponding station-distance from the epicentre. The sum is a value of local magnitude for that seismogram. Since there are two components (EW and NS) of Wood Anderson seismograph, average of the two magnitude values may be taken as the station magnitude. Then average of all the station magnitudes is an estimate of the local magnitude M_L for the earthquake.

A graphical procedure for estimating the Richter magnitude (M_L) is then developed; it is exemplified in Fig. 2.7. The S-P time and the maximum trace amplitude on the seismogram are used to obtain M_L = 5.0 in this example. In Richter's procedure, the largest amplitude recorded on the seismogram is taken.

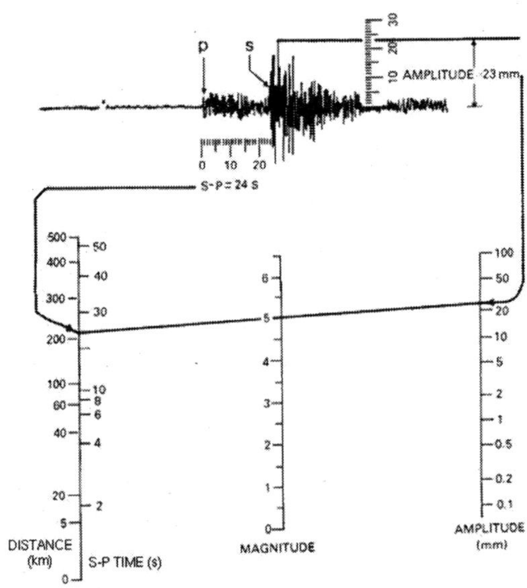

Fig. 2.7 Example of estimating Richter magnitude (M_L) of a local earthquake. Procedure: measure the S-P interval (=24 seconds), maximum amplitude (= 23 mm), and draw a straight line between the appropriate points on the distance (left) and amplitude (right) scales to obtain M_L = 5.0 (Bolt, 1999).

It follows from its definition that there is no upper or lower limit in the magnitude scale. The size of an earthquake is, however, limited by the strength of rocks in the Earth's crust. The maximum size of an earthquake that has been recorded in south Asia is 8.9 in the Richter magnitude scale (December 26, 2004 Sumatra earthquake, IMD report, 2005). The Richter magnitude, however, gets saturated at this level. In such cases moment magnitude may be more stable, and the moment magnitude of the Sumatra earthquake was estimated to 9.3. The moment magnitude scale is discussed below.

Body Wave Magnitude (m_b)

It is now a routine practice in seismology to measure the amplitude of the P-wave which is not affected by the focal depth, and thereby determine P-wave or body-wave magnitude (m_b). Gutenberg (1945a) defined body-wave magnitude m_b for teleseismic body waves P and PP in the period range 0.5 to 12 s:

$$m_b = \log (A/T) - f(\Delta, h) \qquad (2.4)$$

where A/T is amplitude-to-period ratio in micrometres per second, and $f(\Delta, h)$ is a calibration function of epicentral distance Δ in degree and focal depth h in kilometre. Gutenberg and Richter (1956) published a table for the calibration function.

It is recommended that the largest amplitude be taken within the first few cycles instead of considering the whole P-wave train (Willmore, 1979). Both the ISC and NEIC, however, determine body wave magnitude only from vertical component short period P-wave readings of $T \leq 3$ s.

Surface Wave Magnitude (M_s)

For shallow and distant earthquakes, a surface wave train is present that is used for estimation of surface wave magnitude M_s. Gutenberg (1945b) defined the surface wave magnitude M_s as:

$$M_s = \log A_{Hmax} - \log Ao\ (\Delta^o) \qquad (2.5)$$

where A_{Hmax} is the maximum combined horizontal ground amplitude in micrometres for surface waves with a period (T) of 20 ± 2 second, and (–log Ao) is a calibration function that is tabulated as a function of epicentral distance Δ in degrees in a similar manner to that for local magnitude (Richter, 1958).

In a collaborative research Karnik et al. (1962) proposed a new M_s scale as below:

$$M_s = \log (A/T)_{max} + 1.66 \log \Delta + 3.3 \qquad (2.6)$$

for epicentral distances $2° < \Delta < 160°$ and source depth $h < 50$ km. The IASPEI committee on magnitudes recommended at its Zurich meeting in 1967 the use of this formula as standard for M_s determination for shallow seismic events ($h \leq 50$ km). Today, both ISC and NEIC use this eq. (2.6) for determination of M_s. The ISC accepts surface waves with period 10-60 s from stations at a distance range 20°-160°.

A difficulty in using the surface-wave magnitude-scale is that it can be applied only for the shallow earthquakes that generate observable surface-waves. For shallow focus earthquakes, an approximate relation between m_b for P-waves and M_s is given by:

$$m_b = 2.5 + 0.63\ M_s \tag{2.7}$$

Moment Magnitude (M_w)

There are some problems that have been encountered with the magnitude scales. For large earthquakes the Richter as well as body wave magnitude scales saturate. No matter how large the earthquake is, the magnitude computed from body waves tend not to get much above 6.0 to 6.5. The surface-wave scale is less affected by this problem, but for very large earthquakes M>8 the surface-wave scale also gets saturated. It turns out that the limitation is in the instrument recording the earthquake. As new long period instruments as well as digital seismographs have come into use, it has been possible to assign a better measure of the size of these very large earthquakes using the moment magnitude scale. Hanks and Kanamori (1979) proposed the moment magnitude scale by:

$$M_w = 2/3 \log M_o - 10.7 \tag{2.8}$$

where M_o is *seismic moment* of the earthquake in dyne cm. The seismic moment is defined as

$$M_o = \mu A\ \Delta u \tag{2.9}$$

where μ = shear modulus, A = fault area and Δu = average slip over the fault area (Aki, 1966).

Hence the seismic moment of an earthquake is a direct measure of the strength of an earthquake caused by fault slip. If an earthquake occurs with surface faulting, we may estimate its rupture length L and average slip Δu. The source area A may be approximated by Lh where h is the focal depth. A reasonable estimate for μ is 3×10^{11} dynes/cm^2. With these quantities we can estimate the seismic moment from eq. 2.9. For more discussion on seismic moment readers may refer to Brune (1976) and Aki and Richards (1980).

The moment magnitude scale is consistent with M_L: 3-6, M_s: 5-8. The moment magnitude M_w has the advantages that it does not saturate at the top of the scale, and it has a sound theoretical basis than M_L or M_s. However, for moderate magnitude shallow focus damaging earthquakes, it is sufficient for engineering purposes to take M_L, M_s and M_w to be roughly the same.

Duration Magnitude (M_d)

Analog paper or film recordings have limited dynamic range. These records are often clipped for strong or even medium magnitude local seismic events. This makes magnitude determination from A_{max} impossible. Therefore, alternative magnitude scale such as M_d was developed. This scale is based on signal duration. It is almost routinely used in microearthquake surveys. Details of this scale is given in Section 3.15.

Macroseismic Magnitude (M_{ms})

Macroseismic magnitudes (M_{ms}) are particularly important for analysis and statistical treatment of historical earthquakes, and were initially proposed by Kawasumi (1951). There are three main ways to compute M_{ms}:

(i) M_{ms} is derived from maximum reported intensity as:

$$M_{ms} = a\ Io + b \tag{2.10}$$

or when focal depth (h) is known

$$M_{ms} = c\ Io + \log h + d \tag{2.11}$$

(ii) M_{ms} is derived from the total area (A) of perceptibility as:

$$M_{ms} = e \log A_{Ii} + f \tag{2.12}$$

where A_{Ii} in km^2 shaken by intensities I_i with $i \geq III$, and a, b, c and d are constants.

Examples of regionally best fitting relationships are published for California (Toppozada, 1975), Italy (Tinti et al., 1987), Australia (Greenhalgh et al., 1989). For Europe Karnik (1969) reported the best results using

$$M_{ms} = 0.5\ I_o + \log h + 0.35 \tag{2.13}$$

(iii) Another M_{ms} is related to the product $P = Io \times A\ (km^2)$, which is independent of the focal depth (Galanopolous, 1961):

$$M_{ms} = \log P + 0.2\ (\log P - 6) \tag{2.14}$$

Magnitude and Frequency of Earthquake Occurrence

As discussed in Chapter 1, the frequency-magnitude relation is a widely accepted concept in seismology. The frequency of earthquake occurrence as a function of magnitude is represented by Gutenberg and Richter (1941) relation:

$$\log_{10} N = a - bM \tag{2.15}$$

where N is the cumulative number of earthquakes of magnitude M or greater, and *a* and *b* are numerical constants. The constant *a* represents the seismic level of activity; it is not an independent quantity. It depends upon the largest magnitude in the given group of earthquakes and on the constant *b*. The constant *b* describes the rate of increase of earthquakes as magnitude decreases. Studies in many areas of the world have shown that the *b-values* are usually within the range of 0.5-1.5 (e.g. Pacheco et al., 1992; Wiemer et al., 1998). This range corresponds to an increase in number of earthquakes 4 to 16 times for each decrease of magnitude by one unit. For a given sample of earthquake magnitude data, if we plot $\log_{10}$ N versus M, the *b-value* can be estimated from the slope of the log-linear relation, the least-square fit line. The relation equally holds good for a aftershock sequence (Utsu, 1961 and 1969).

Readers interested in more detailed discussion on b-value estimation and its significance in earthquake statistics are referred to Utsu (1965), Aki (1965), Shi and Bolt (1982), Frohlich and Davis (1993) and Wiemer and Wyss (1997). A detailed study of b-value in northeast India region is given in Chapter 6.

2.4.2 Earthquake Intensity

Rossi-Forel Intensity Scale

The first intensity scale of modern times was developed by De Rossi of Italy and Forel of Switzerland in 1880s. This scale, which is still sometimes used in describing damage effect of an earthquake, has values I to X. The 1906 San Francisco earthquake was rated with the Rossi-Forel intensity scale. For description of this scale readers are referred to Richter (1958).

Modified Mercalli (MM) Intensity Scale (1956 version)

The Italian seismologist and volcanologist Mercalli made certain changes in the Rossi-Forel scale in 1902. Cancani and Sieberg made further changes to develop Mercalli-Cancani-Sieberg (MCS) scale in 1923, and the scale was expanded to 12 degrees i.e. I to XII. Wood and Neumann gave a new version of the MCS scale, which came in use in USA as Modified Mercalli (MM) Scale. Richter (1958) gave a rewritten version of the MM scale, which is referred to MM scale (1956 version). Like the Richter scale for estimating M_L, the Modified Mercalli (MM) scale is popularly used for estimating the earthquake shaking intensity. The 1956 version of this scale is given in Appendix 2.1.

Medvedev-Sponheuer-Karnik (MSK) Intensity Scale (1992 Version)

The MCS and MM scales were thoroughly revised and the MSK scale was approved at the UNESCO meeting on Seismology and Engineering in 1964 in Paris. Later it was, however, realised that introduction of the sophisticated MSK scale would be of less practical use. A working group, European Seismological Commission (ESC), was established in 1988 for logical version of the MSK scale. A modified version of the scale was finalised and adopted as MSK scale at the XXIII ESC General Assembly in 1992 in Prague.

The MSK and MM scales are almost equivalent, only difference is in the sophistication employed in the formulation. It may, however, be noted that although these scales have 12 degrees, in practice only 8 degree scales are used. Intensity I means not felt and intensity II is too weak to be reported; so, these two ratings are rarely used. At the other end of the scale, intensity XII is defined in a manner which cannot necessarily be reached in an earthquake. Again intensities X and XI are hard to differentiate in practice; so, intensity XI is rarely used. Thus the working range of these scales is usually from intensity III to intensity X.

In the macroseismic study of an earthquake, the following simple steps are followed:

(i) *Data acquisition*: This may be done by questionnaire survey, field visit, appeals for information, literature search or by other means.
(ii) *Data sorting*: The data may be organised into a form in which it can be interpreted. This may be done by arranging the questionnaire indicating the place of origin.
(iii) *Intensity assignment*: Data are interpreted using the intensity scale, and a table indicating places with intensities may be prepared.

Isoseismals

Isoseismals are the curved lines joining the localities of same intensity. Isoseismals often show elliptical elongation in the direction of major structural trends/damage. Generally the areas, the *isoseists,* between the isoseismals are marked with intensity numbers (say IV or V), and the curved lines are drawn to separate out the isoseists. An old practice was to assume epicentre, in absence of seismographs, in the centre of *meizoseismal* area i.e. in the maximum intensity zone. Since the inception of the instrumental seismology, such practice is, however, discontinued. It is rather observed that instrumentally located epicentre is mostly outside the meizoseismal area. Isoseismal maps for the great Indian earthquakes are exemplified in Sec. 2.7. The geologists look at an isoseismal map with a view point of nature and extent of faulting. The engineer's interest in such map is to judge the performance of various types of construction under such conditions. An isoseismal map becomes an index of weak or danger spots to be avoided for future construction or warrant safety measures.

Intensity and Acceleration

Richter (1958) has given an empirical relation between intensity and acceleration of an earthquke as follows:

$$\log a = \frac{I}{3} - \frac{1}{2} \tag{2.16}$$

where a is the acceleration in cm/sec^2 and I is the MM intensity. If one assumes $I = 1\frac{1}{2}$ which represents the limit of perceptibility between I and II, then $\log a = 0$, or $a = 1$ cm/sec^2. Such an acceleration may reach the level of shaking ordinarily perceptible to persons. Similarly, if one lets $I = 7\frac{1}{2}$, then log $a = 2$ or $a = 100$ cm/sec^2 which is equal to 0.1g approximately. This value is appreciable as it damages ordinary structures not designed to be resistant. One gets $a = 1$ g, for $I = 10\frac{1}{2}$, which is rather rare.

2.4.3 Earthquake Energy

It is tempting to correlate the *energy release* of an earthquake with its *magnitude* or *intensity*. Although the correspondence is very approximate, it is nevertheless very useful for estimating the amount of energy released by an earthquake.

Gutenberg and Richter's (1954) elaborate calculations produced the formula which relates energy release with magnitude as follows:

$$\log E = 12 + 1.8\ M \tag{2.17}$$

This relation is fair enough for the earthquakes of magnitude range $4 < M < 7$, but for the large earthquakes, energy given by this formula is too high. Gutenberg and Richter (1956) revised the formula after extensive study of strong motion seismograms, and preferred unified magnitude m derived from body waves recorded at teleseismic distances, and it took the form:

$$\log E = 5.8 + 2.4\ m \tag{2.18}$$

where $m = 2.5 + 0.63\ M_s$, thus it is equivalent to

$$\log E = 11.4 + 1.5\ M_s \tag{2.19}$$

Putting M = 8, eqs 2.17 and 2.19 give log E = 26.4 and 23.4 respectively. Thus the revised relation (eq. 2.19) greatly reduced the values of energy for the larger shocks ($M > 7$).

Shebalin (1955) derived formulas to relate earthquake energy, intensity and depth as follows:

$$0.9 \log E - I = 3.8 \log h - 3.3 \tag{2.20}$$

and $$0.9 \log E - I = 3.1 \log h - 4.4 \tag{2.21}$$

where h is the hypocentral depth in kilometres and I is the maximum intensity (MM scale) at the surface. Equation 2.20 applies to hypocentres from the surface down to 70 km, and eq. 2.21 to depth of 80 km or more.

It is worth noting, mainly of journalistic interest, that an official figure for the energy release by a nominal atom bomb of the Hiroshima type is 8×10^{20} ergs, and a great earthquake ($M \geq 8$) might have an energy of 8×10^{26} ergs, which is comparable with million atom bombs. Since the energy of the annual *heat flow* from the interior of the Earth is roughly 8×10^{27} ergs, the two numbers are close enough to suggest various geophysical speculations. Revision for seismic energy release now gives a figure 9×10^{24} ergs per year, which is hardly more than a thousandth of the heat energy. Table 2.1

illustrates changes in ground motion and energy with magnitude change. It shows, for example, that a magnitude 7.0 earthquake produces 10 times more ground motion than a magnitude 6.0 earthquake, but it releases 32 times more energy. The energy release best indicates the destructive power of an earthquake.

Table 2.1: Magnitude versus ground motion and energy

Magnitude Change	*Ground Motion Change (Displacement)*	*Energy Change*
1.0	10.0 times	about 32 times
0.5	3.2 times	about 5.5 times
0.3	2.0 times	about 3 times
0.1	1.3 times	about 1.4 times

It can be shown that a magnitude 9.7 earthquake is 794 times bigger on a seismogram than a magnitude 6.8 earthquake. The magnitude scale is logarithmic, so

$$10^{9.7}/10^{6.8} = 10^{9.7-6.8} = 10^{2.9} = 794.328 \tag{2.22}$$

The magnitude scale is really comparing amplitudes of waves on a seismogram, not the energy of the earthquakes. So, a magnitude 9.7 is 794 times bigger than a M 6.8 earthquake as measured on seismograms, but the M 9.7 earthquake is about 23,500 times STRONGER than that of the M 6.8! This means that it would take about 23,500 earthquakes of magnitude 6.8 to equal the energy released by one magnitude 9.7 earthquake. Since it is really the energy or strength that knocks down buildings, this is really the more important comparison. This explains why big earthquakes are so much devastating than small ones. The amplitude ("size") differences are big enough, but the energy ("strength") differences are huge.

2.5 SOME USEFUL DEFINITIONS IN EARTHQUAKE SEISMOLOGY

As stated in the introduction of this chapter, earthquake seismology being a dual science some useful terms are defined here from the view point of geologist investigating the earthquake effect in the field and the geophysicist/ seismologist interpreting the instrumental records of their observatory/field survey in the laboratory.

Accelerometer is a seismograph that records acceleration as a function of time. The c.g.s. unit of acceleration is the Gal (= 1 centimetre per second per second), one thousandth of a Gal is a *milliGal.* Acceleration of earthquake motion is expressed in terms of g (g = acceleration due to gravity = 980 cm/ sec^2). A *strong-motion seismograph,* which does not record continuously, is triggered into motion by the first wave of an earthquake above threshold intensity. These instruments are designed to trigger during strong acceleration of the ground, and continues for some minutes or until the ground shaking falls again to the imperceptible levels. The acceleration of earthquake motion or g value is obtained from this record, which is a very useful parameter for earthquake engineers for assigning design factor of engineering construction.

Asperity is defined as a strong section of a fault system, that is locked during the decades of stress build up in the fault system, and it releases most of its energy during an eventful earthquake. The surrounding areas, *barriers,* are weakly coupled, possibly drag along during an earthquake. The effective stress normal to the fault surface in asperity is believed to be relatively higher than in the barrier. Alternatively, barriers may be regions of ductile deformation in which rupture dies out. This type of barrier is known as *relaxation barrier. Aseismic creep,* i.e. continuous slip on a fault, may also produce relaxation barrier surrounding an asperity, that limit the rupture dimension when the asperity fails. The best known *creeping fault* is the 100 km long segment of the San Andreas between San Juan and Parkfiled, California. Faults that creep require special frictional behaviour; either the fault has unusually low normal stresses or the fault is lined with very ductile or weak materials, the *fault gouge.*

Asthenosphere is the layer below the lithosphere (Fig. 2.2). The asthenosphere is marked by low seismic velocity and high seismic attenuation. It is a soft layer, probably partially molten. *Lithosphere* is the outer rigid shell, and consists of crust and the upper mantle.

Compression and dilatation, corresponding to the nature of Primary (P) seismic-waves, refer to the direction of the first arrival of P-wave on a seismogram. Conventionally, for vertical component seismometer, upward motion indicates a compression of the ground, and downward motion a dilatation. When the source of P-wave is a small explosion at a point in the Earth the first P-wave generated would push outward on a spherical surface, and the seismographs would detect this P-wave as upward movement, referred to as compression. If the P-wave arises from rupture on a fault, as in the case of an earthquake, the first motions will not be all compressions. Depending on the directions in which P-wave left the fault and depending on the positions of the seismographs, both up and down motions of the P-wave would be recorded.

Epicentre and hypocentre indicate the earthquake location. Epicentre is the point on the Earth's surface directly above the focus or hypocentre of an earthquake. Focus or hypocentre is the origin point at which the rupture initiates, and *focal depth* is the depth of the focus below the surface of the Earth (Fig. 2.8). *Origin time* is the instant at which an earthquake commences at the hypocentre, and *transit time* is the elapsed time between the origin time and the arrival of a given seismic wave at a seismograph station. Most researchers term this as *travel time* (more details in Chapter 3).

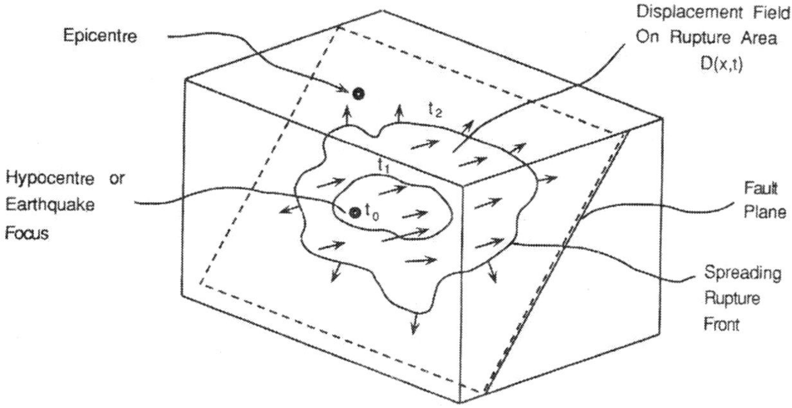

Fig. 2.8 Diagram showing epicentre, focus (hypocentre), rupture area, fault-plane etc. (after Bolt, 1999).

Gravity anomaly is the deviation of the observed acceleration of gravity (g) from an expected value calculated from the general gravitational field of the Earth. Gravity anomaly is expressed in terms of *Free-air anomaly, Bouguer anomaly* and *Isostatic anomaly*. The free-air anomaly takes into consideration of the free-air correction, which compensates for the fact that the attraction of gravity above sea level decreases with height because of the increased distance from the Earth's centre. The residual between the gravity so corrected and the value calculated from the International Formula (which considers latitude) is referred to as free-air anomaly. The *Bouguer anomaly* considers the attraction of the material between the elevation of the observing station and the sea-level, which is called Bouguer correction. The International Formula, however, makes no allowance for lateral variation of density of the Earth's crust. An *Isostatic correction* is made on the basis of surface elevation data. The form of the correction depends on the assumed isostatic model of Airy (1855) or Pratt (1859). Once the data are corrected for predicted isostatic effects along with the free-air and Bouguer corrections, the residual between the observation so corrected and the calculated value at the latitude of the observing station is referred to as the isostatic anomaly. If perfect isostatic compensation exists, the anomaly is zero. If the anomaly is positive over a land, it infers to a deficit of compensation. If it is negative, the area is considered to be over compensated.

Heat flow is the outward flow of Earth's internal heat through the crust. Determination of heat flow involves measurement of temperature gradient in the crust and measurement of thermal conductivities of the rocks in which the gradient is measured. Heat flow unit (HFU) is 10^{-2}cal/m^2 sec. The mean heat flow of the Earth is 1.2-1.5 HFU. Heat flow ranges from about 0.9 in the shield areas to over 2 HFU in the Cenozoic volcanic areas. In mid-ocean ridges the values reach upto 8 HFU. A sinking lithospheric plate, on the

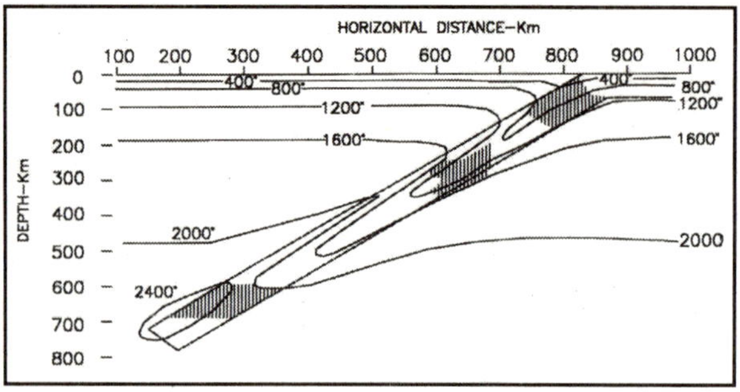

Fig. 2.9 Temperature distribution in a down going plate, shaded areas indicate zone of phase changes (after Toksöz et al., 1971).

other hand, is a very efficient heat sink; the mean heat flow in a sinking plate is of the order of – 10 HFU. Consequently, the continuous sinking of the plate should induce considerable cooling of the surrounding mantle. An example of temperature distribution in a down going plate is shown in Fig. 2.9.

Macroseismic effects of earthquakes are those which are observed on the large scale in the field without any instrumental aid. Earthquake damages, crustal deformations etc. are referred to as macroseismic effects.

Microseismic effects, on the other hand, are those that can be observed in small scale only with instruments. Quite illogically, the term *microseism* is used in a different way. These are not small earthquakes. More or less continuous disturbances or seismic noises in the ground recorded by seismographs are called *microseisms*. Most of these are associated with weather, wind action on topography and in trees, other natural movements such as breaking of surf on the beach etc.

Q factor or quality factor describes the attenuation of seismic waves. It is inverse of attenuation coefficient, and an important parameter in earthquake engineering. *Q* is a dimensionless quantity that expresses the wave amplitude decay, which occurs when a wave propagates through a medium, and is not attributable to geometrical spreading. It is a combination of intrinsic attenuation, the loss of elastic energy to heat or other forms of energy, scattering and deflection and/or mode conversion of seismic energy due to randomly distributed inhomogeneities in the transmitting medium. *Q* values are generally determined from strong-motion accelerograms and broadband seismograms. High seismic velocity and high *Q* values are observed along the sinking lithospheric plate. *Q* is about 500 for the crust, 150 for the upper mantle and 1000 along the sinking plate. A schematic distribution of *Q* in a subduction zone is shown in Fig. 2.10.

Seismograph is an earthquake recording instrument which measures, in details, the ground shaking. The first earthquake recorder was an artistic device invented by a Chinese scholar, Chang Heng, about 132 A.D. (Fig. 2.11). The instrument was a *seismoscope*, unlike seismograph it did not record the complete time history of the earthquake waves but did record the

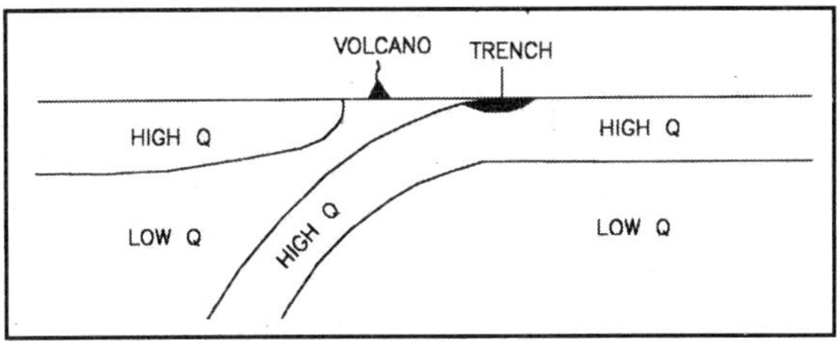

Fig. 2.10 Schematic diagram showing distribution of *Q* (quality factor) in a subduction zone.

Fig. 2.11 Left: photograph showing Chinese scholar Chang Heng with the seismocope he designed (about 132 A.D.). Right: Maori god of earthquake (carving and photo, courtesy: Terry Ball, New Zealand).

direction of principal impulse due to an earthquake. The first effective seismographs were constructed just before the beginning of the twentieth century.

Seismometer is a sensor part of a seismograph. A variety of suitable components (vertical and/or horizontal) high-gain seismometers are now commercially available to meet various network requirements. A brief theory and practice of the seismometers are discussed in Chapter 3. *Seismograms* are the detailed graphical records of the earthquake waves. Photographic, magnetic, pen-ink, micro-film and smoked-paper recordings are common till the development of digital instruments in the recent times.

2.6 EARTHQUAKE EFFECTS AND HAZARDS

2.6.1 Damage to Man-made Structures

Effects of earthquakes on artificial structures are of prime importance to the public, engineers and architects. Description of earthquake damages includes the degree of damage made on small weak mud-hut to modern structures. Masonry structures, however, have been classified into four categories to devise the intensity scale (see Appendix 2.1). Some damages are caused by the effect of shaking not directly on the masonry structure but on the foundation. Warping or fissuring can make a considerable damage even to exceptionally strong building. Relative motions of the two sides of an active fault may destroy a structure of any kind by bending or crushing. Other engineering structures like railways, bridges, dams etc. are also subject to severe damage by shaking, slumping or faulting. Proper earthquake-resistant design for large or tall structures is still vigorously debated in the engineering profession.

Causes of most earthquake-damages are due to the horizontal motion rather than the vertical part of the motion. Vertical motion operates against gravity, whereas horizontal motion meets no such resistance. Earthquake effects are often evaluated exclusively in terms of acceleration. With an amplitude of one inch and a frequency of one per second, we have an acceleration of 0.1g, which is considered as damaging. If such motion continues only few seconds, it will not damage ordinary structure, but if the motion continues for 15 or 20 seconds, as it may in a great earthquake, damage may be much greater. Long duration, reasonably high acceleration and considerable amplitudes are the combination which cause maximum damage in buildings and loss of lives. Some killing earthquakes of the world are tabulated in Table 2.2.

Table 2.2: Some killing earthquakes of the world: 1500-2005 (compiled from Utsu, 2002)

Year, Month & Date	*Region*	*Magnitude/Intensity*	*Loss of Lives*
1	2	3	4
1500, January 04	China (Yunnan)	7.0, X	10,000
1509, September 14	Turkey	7.4, XI	13,000
1531, January 26	Lisbon Portugal		30,000
1549, February 16	Qayin, Iran	6.7, IX	3,000
1556, January 23	Shanxi, China	8.3	830,000
1570, February 08	Chile	8.3, XI	2,000
1575, December 16	Chile	8.5, X	1,500
1605, February 03	Japan	7.9	1,000
1605, July 13	China	7.5, XI	1,000
1611, September 27	Japan	6.9, IX	3,700
1611, December 02	Japan	8.1	5,000
1622, October 25	China	7.0, X	12,000
1626, June 28	China	7.0, IX	5,200
1627, July 30	Italy	6.8, X^+	5,000
1639, March 27	Italy	6.9, XI	30,000

(Contd.)

The above equations (eqs 2.33-2.35) determine *travel-time curves.* Figure 2.34 shows the travel-time curves for principal rays for the layered structure in Fig. 2.33. The direct and reflected arrivals exist only at short distances. The direct arrival is described by a straight line with a slope $dT/dx = p = 1/V_1$. The reflected arrival time is described by a hyperbola. The intercept, at $X = 0$, has a travel time $2h/V_1$. At large distances, the branch of the reflected travel-time curve becomes asymptotic to the direct arrival.

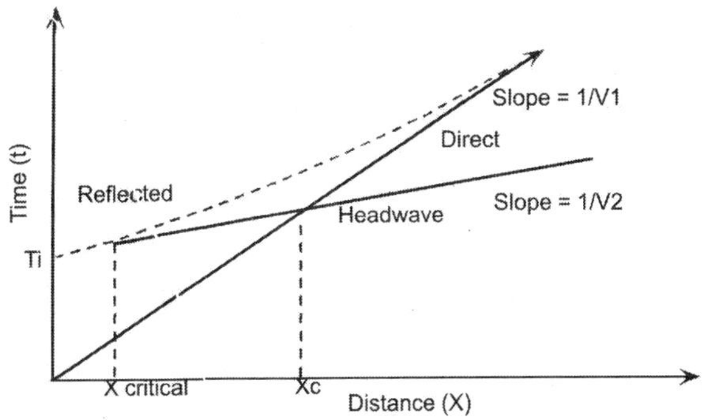

Fig. 2.34 Travel-time curves for the three primary rays in a two-layer velocity structure (Fig. 2.33).

The head wave travel-time curve represents a straight line with a slope $dT/dx = p = 1/V_2$. The head wave travels with a faster velocity, and eventually becomes the first arrival. The direct arrival is the first arrival until the *cross over distance*, X_c, after which the head wave becomes the first arrival. The cross over distance or critical distance, X_c, can be estimated by visualizing that at X_c the travel times of the direct wave and head wave are equal, i.e.

$$T_{\text{direct}} = T_{\text{head}}$$

or,
$$\frac{X_c}{V_1} = \frac{X_c}{V_2} + \frac{2h}{\cos i_c} \cdot \frac{1}{V_1} \tag{2.36}$$

or,
$$X_c = 2h \left[\frac{V_2 + V_1}{V_2 - V_1} \right]^{1/2}$$

The travel time curve in Fig. 2.34 is, however, not complete because we have only considered three rays. There will be many rays, and the seismograms are mixtures of P and S waves, converted phases and multiple reflections. The importance of travel-time curve is its interpretative power, and we can determine the layer velocities and layer thicknesses.

The depth to the interface or crustal thickness (h) can be calculated from the cross over distance (X_c) as shown in equation 2.36. The crustal thickness can also be estimated from the intercept time (T_i):

$$h = \frac{T_i}{2} \cdot \frac{V_1 V_2}{\left(V_2^2 - V_2^2\right)^{1/2}} \tag{2.37}$$

The intercept time T_i can be determined graphically.

2.16.2 Multi-layer Case

The time-depth relation derived for a two-layered media can readily be extrapolated to apply to a large number of layers as long as the velocity in each layer is higher than in the one just above it. The general equation may be written as

$$T = px + 2\sum_{i=1}^{n} h_i n_i \tag{2.38}$$

Figure 2.35 illustrates ray paths and time-distance curves for each media; the lower most designated for generality as n^{th}. The travel-time curve shows many branches due to head waves at each interface.

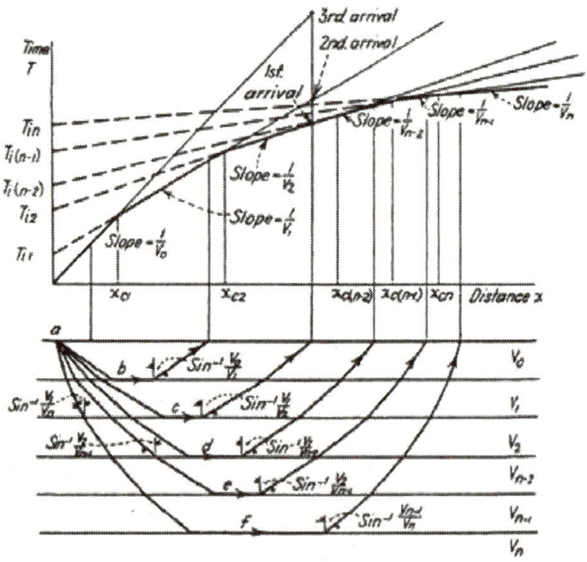

Fig. 2.35 Ray paths and travel-time curves for finely layered Earth (Lay and Wallace, 1995).

Low Velocity Layer and Blind Zone

We may mention two special cases, which complicate the interpretation of travel-time curves. First of these is the presence of a low velocity layer. Figure 2.36 shows that the velocity of layer 2 is less than that of layer 1 and the half space. In such case no *head wave* occurs along the interface between the layers 1 and 2. One would estimate a *pseudo thickness* of a single layer with velocity V_1 over a half space of velocity V_3. This would result in an over estimate of the actual depth to the half space.

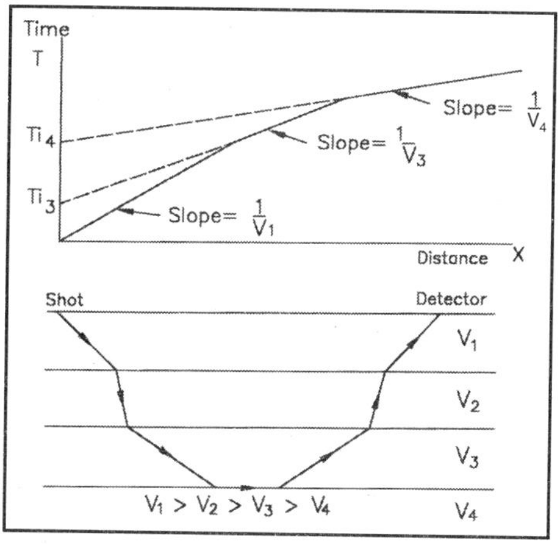

Fig. 2.36 Ray paths for a structure with a low velocity layer, no head wave at the interface V_1 and V_2.

The second special case is the *blind zone,* which is caused by a thin layer or low velocity contrast. The layer may be so thin that the head wave from it is never a first arrival. This may also happen if V_2/V_1 is not much larger than 1. One of the practical examples of blind zone is the *Conrad discontinuity* in the crust.

Increase of Velocity with Depth

Travel-time curves in a continuous medium, i.e. with continuous velocity distribution, shows subtle differences in the character of the travel-time curves (Fig. 2.37). The slowness ($1/V$) observed at a distance X can be found by taking the slope $p = dt/dx$ or tangent of the travel-time curve.

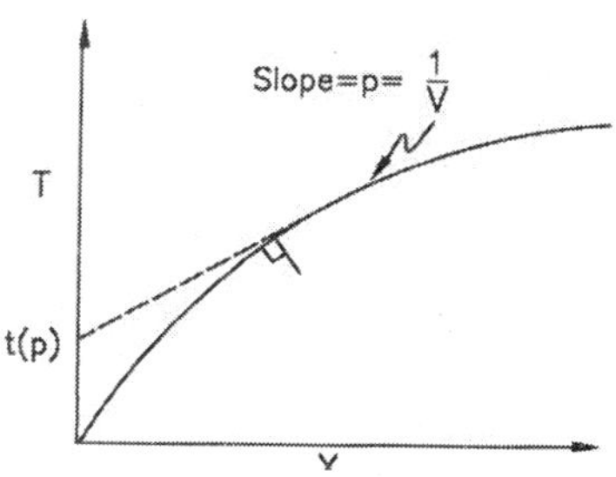

Fig. 2.37 Travel-time curve in a continuous velocity structure.

Dipping Layer

Travel-time curve for *dipping layer* is again complicated; it depends whether the rays are travelling up-dip or down-dip; Fig. 2.38 shows ray-geometry and corresponding travel-time curves. The direct arrivals have the same slowness, but the head waves have different apparent velocities where:

$$\frac{1}{V_u} = \frac{\sin(i_c - \theta)}{V_1} \tag{2.39}$$

and $$\frac{1}{V_d} = \frac{\sin(i_c + \theta)}{V_1}$$

The resulting travel-time equation can be written as

$$T_u = \frac{2h_2 \cos i_c \cos\theta}{V_1} + \frac{X \sin(i_c - \theta)}{V_1} \tag{2.40}$$

$$T_d = \frac{2h_1 \cos i_c \cos\theta}{V_1} + \frac{X \sin(i_c + \theta)}{V_1} \tag{2.41}$$

where u and d represent up-dip and down-dip observations respectively. It may be noted that the cross over distance is larger for up-dip travel paths. The total travel time for the source-receiver geometry is, however, the same because of reciprocity for interchanged source and receiver locations.

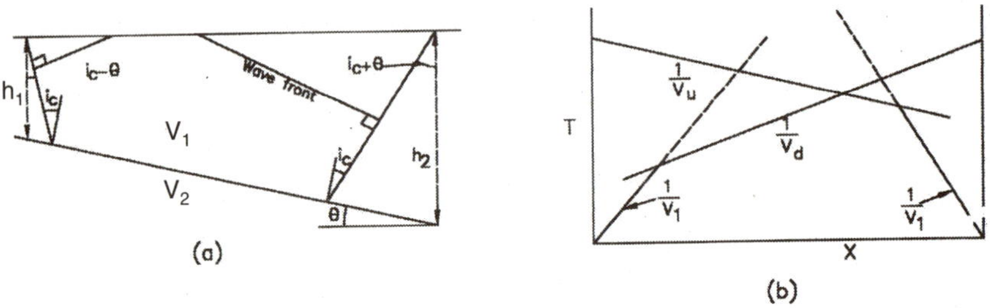

Fig. 2.38 (a) Ray geometry for head wave along a dipping interface. (b) Travel-time curves (up-dip) and down-dip for the dipping structure.

2.17 TELESEISMIC WAVES AND INTERIOR OF THE EARTH

Virtually all our direct informations about the interior of the Earth are derived from the observations of earthquake generated seismic waves only. Since much of the Earth is an elastic solid, two kinds of body waves can propagate through the Earth. The path of the waves are affected by two main discontinuities in the Earth; one at a depth of 30-60 km, and the other at a depth of 2900 km. The first one is called the *Moho discontinuity,* which is of special importance in interpreting seismograms at short epicentral distances upto a few hundred kilometres as discussed above. Evidence of the second discontinuity was discovered by Wiechert and by Oldham in 1906, but precise identification and determination of depth of this discontinuity was made by Gutenberg (1914), hence called *Gutenberg discontinuity*. These two discontinuities divide the Earth internally into an outer shell, called the *crust*, an intermediate shell, called the *mantle*, and a central *core*. The major divisions of the Earth's interior are shown in Fig. 2.39. The mantle is subdivided into upper mantle and lower mantle, and core is subdivided into outer core and inner core.

(a)

(b)

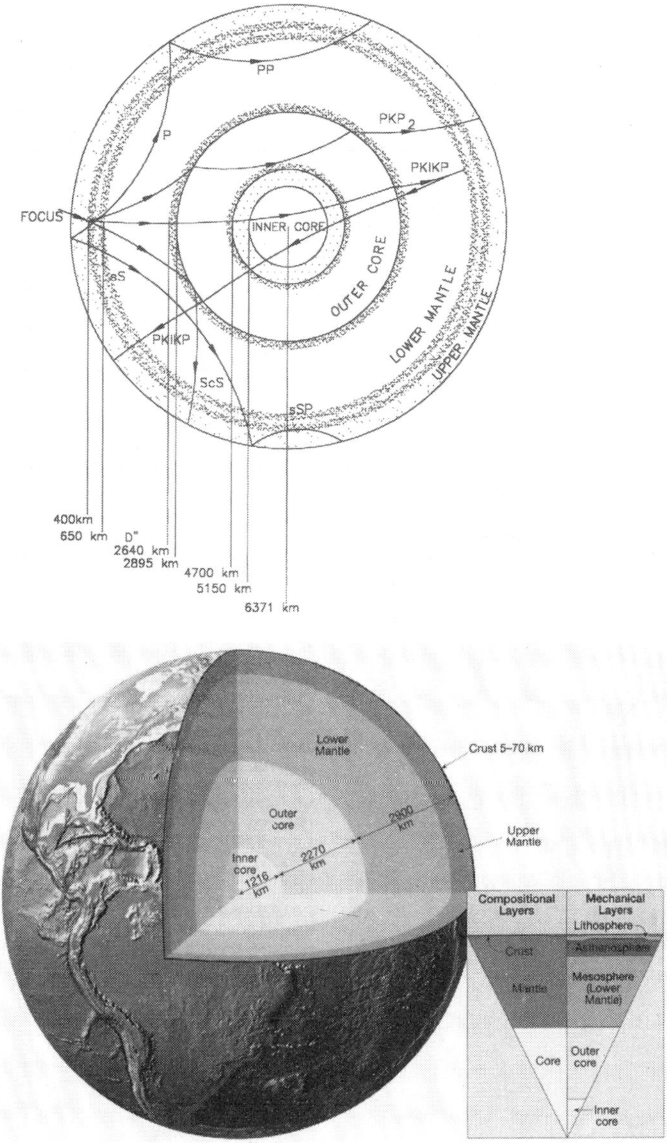

Fig. 2.39 (a) Interior of the Earth and seismic waves which penetrate mantle, core or inner core (modified from Garland, 1979). (b) 3-D view of the interior of the Earth (Courtesy: Roger Masson, U.K.).

Seismic waves arriving at a distance beyond 10° up to about 30° mainly travel through the upper mantle (Moho to 410 km) and through the transition zone to the lower mantle (410-660 km). The strong discontinuities in the transition zone have strong *seismic impedance* (i.e. the quantity $V \times \rho$, that increases with the increase of velocity V and density ρ). This results triplications of the travel-time curve for P waves and S waves, that gives rise to complicated short-period waveforms consisting of sequence of successive onsets with different amplitudes. The base of the transition zone, between the lower mantle and outer core, is labelled as D″ region (Bullen, 1965) (Fig. 2.39a), which may be caused by either chemical differentiation in the mantle or by chemical reactions between core and mantle (e.g. Lay, 1989; Jeanloz, 1990).

At epicentral distances between about 30° and 100°, the P and S waves travel through the lower mantle that is characterized by a rather smooth positive velocity and density gradient. The seismograms are clearly structured with P and S arrivals, followed by multiple surface and core-mantle boundary (CMB) reflections on conversions (Fig. 2.39a). The existence of the great velocity reduction across the CMB causes seismic wave energy to diffract into the geometric shadow zone at distances greater than 100°.

Beyond 100°, only P-wave enters outer core, and reaches surface. There is a dramatic reduction of P-wave velocity, from 13.7 km/s in the lower most mantle to 8.0 km/s in the upper outer core. This P-wave forms a core shadow. Oldham (1906) first observed that a P-wave arriving at the antipodes of an earthquake was late, in comparison with the expected arrival time. He proposed the existence of core of lower velocity than outer region, and predicted the presence of a *shadow zone*. Gutenberg (1914) verified that there was a shadow zone for P between $\Delta = 103°$ and $\Delta = 142°$ with strong arrivals just beyond 142° (Fig. 2.40). Gutenberg estimated the depth to the core boundary as 2900 km, which stood unchallenged until very recently. The shadow zone of the core is not complete, there being arrivals of P-waves of small amplitude through the entire zone. Lehmann (1935) suggested that these arise from *inner core* of higher velocity within the main core. Her proposal of inner core became widely accepted.

The teleseismic arrivals, corresponding to different paths, are illustrated in Fig. 2.39a. The letters P and S are used to designate reflected or refracted waves outside the core. The subscripts **c** and **i** denote reflections from the

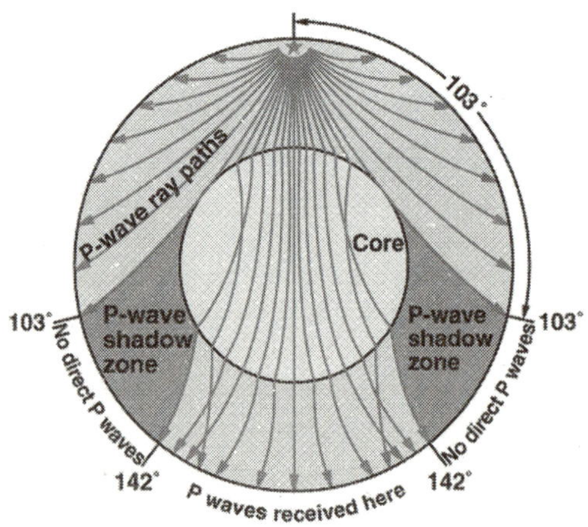

Fig. 2.40 Ray paths of the P-wave through interior of the Earth, showing the shadow zone.

outer and inner core boundaries respectively, while the letters **K** and **I** indicate P waves through outer and inner core. A wave of S type through the outer core has not been observed. We have also phases such as PP, reflected from the Earth's surface. Table 2.4 gives details of different local, regional and teleseismic phases. For global earthquakes and global seismology, readers may refer to Lay and Wallace (1995).

Table 2.4: Nomenclature of Seismic Phases (Kuthánek, 1990)

Symbol	*Meaning*
Local and regional events	
P, S	Direct compressional or shear wave travelling through the upper crust (observed only at very short epicentral distances)
P_g, S_g	Compressional or shear wave in the granitic layer of the crust
P_mP, S_mS	Compressional or shear wave reflected at Moho
P_n, S_n	Compressional or shear wave travelling along (just beneath) the Moho discontinuity, so-called head wave
P^*, S^* (or P_b, S_b)	Compressional or shear wave travelling along (just beneath) the Conrad discontinuity
pP_n	Depth phase that leaves the focus upward as *P*, is reflected as *P* at the free surface and continues further as P_n
sP_n	Depth phase that leaves the focus upward as *S*, is reflected and converted into *P* at the free surface and continues further as S_n
R_g	Short-period crustal surface wave of Rayleigh type
L_g	Guided crustal wave traversing large distances along continental paths
T	Compressional wave propagating through the ocean (Tertiary wave). *T* phases are occasionally observed even at larger teleseismic distances
TP_g (TS_g, TR_g)	Wave that travels the ocean and land portion of the total transmission path as *T* and P_g (S_g, R_g), respectively
Teleseismic events	
P, S	Direct compressional or shear wave, so-called elementary or main wave
PP, PPP, SS, SSS	*P* or *S* wave reflected once or twice at the Earth's surface
SP	*S* wave converted into P upon reflection at the Earth's surface
PPS, PSP, PSS	*P* wave twice reflected/converted at the Earth's surface.
PcP, ScS	*P* or *S* wave reflected at the core-mantle boundary
PcS, ScP	*P* or *S* wave converted respectively into *S* or *P* upon reflection at the core-mantle boundary
pP, pS, pPP, pPS, etc.	Depth phase that leaves the focus upward as *P*(*p* leg), is reflected/converted at the free surface and continues further as *P*, *S*, *PP*, *PS*, etc.

(*Contd.*)

Table 2.4 (*Contd.*)

Symbol	*Meaning*
sP, sS, sPP, sPS, etc.	Depth phase that leaves the focus upward as *S*(*s* leg), is reflected/converted at the free surface and continues further as *P, S, PP, PS*, etc.
pmP	*P* wave reflected at the underside of Moho
pwP	*P* wave reflected at the water surface
PdP	*P* wave reflected at the underside of a discontinuity at depth *d* in the upper part of the Earth. *d* is given in kilometres, e.g., *P400P*
Pc, Sc or *Pdif, Sdif*	*P* or *S* wave that is diffracted around the core-mantle boundary
PKP (or *P′*)	*P* wave traversing the outer core
PKS	*P* wave traversing the outer core as *P* and converted back into *S* when again entering the mantle
SKS	*S* wave converted into *S* on refraction when leaving the core
SKP	*S* wave converted into *P* on refraction into the outer core
PKP1, PKP2 or PKP_{BC}, PKP_{AB}	Different branches of *PKP*
PKIKP or P^2, $PKPr_{DF}$	*P* wave traversing the outer and inner core
PKiKP	*P* wave reflected at the boundary of the inner core
PKIIKP	*P* wave reflected from the inside of the inner-core boundary
PKKP	*P* wave reflected from the inside of the core-mantle boundary
PmKP (*m* = 3, 4,...)	*P* wave reflected m – 1 times from the inside of the core-mantle boundary
SmKS (*m* = 3, 4,...)	*S* wave converted into *P* on refraction at the outer core, reflected m – 1 times from the inside of the core-mantle boundary and finally converted back into *S* when again entering the mantle
PKPPKP (or *P′ P′*)	*PKP* wave reflected from the free surface, passing twice through the core
P′dP′	*PKP* reflected at the underside of the discontinuity at depth *d* in the upper part of the Earth, *d* is given in kilometers
LR	Surface wave of Rayleigh type
LQ	Surface wave of Love type
G	Mantle wave of Love type
R	Mantle wave of Rayleigh type
G1, G2	*LQ*-type mantle wave that travels the direct and anticentre routes. Waves that have, in addition, travelled once or several times around the Earth are denoted *G3, G4, G5, G6*, etc.
R1, R2	*LR*-type mantle wave that travels the direct and anticentre routes. Waves that have, in addition, travelled once or several times around the Earth are denoted *R3, R4, R5, R6*, etc.

Global Travel-time Models

The velocities of P and S waves provide information about the Earth's interior. When an earthquake occurs, waves from it are recorded at known locations and at known times, although the latter is not free of error. The travel-time curves are always plotted against the arc distance (Δ). The time interval S-P measured at any station gives a unique indication of arc distance to the earthquake, and distances determined from three or more stations locate the source uniquely within limited errors. The weakness in this method is, however, a time-distance curve must be established before the source can be located, but this location is essential for construction of the curve. So, in the early history of seismology time-distance curve was constructed for the earthquakes, which were precisely located by direct observations or by very close seismographs (Wiechert and Zöppritz, 1907).

Revision of time-distance curves was accomplished by Jeffreys (1935) by least-square technique. In this method, the residuals i.e. the differences between the observed arrival times of P or S and their computed arrival times based on preliminary location and preliminary travel-time curves, are minimized by simultaneous adjustment of epicentre coordinates, origin time and travel-time curve. Number of equations become very great as more earthquakes and stations are utilised. However, Jeffreys devised a method of treating the observations in groups. This analysis in collaboration with Bullen produced the Jeffreys-Bullen (J-B) Tables (1935, 1940). This gives adjusted travel times for P and S waves and also for reflected and refracted waves as functions of the arc distances Δ (Fig. 2.41). Bullen (1965) has described the production of these tables, including the derivation of the correction for the elliptical shape of the Earth. This has provided basic information of body wave seismology, which in turn yielded Earth models that are still taken as standards for reference. Improvement in observational technique, specially timing and availability of large artificial known explosions, have permitted correction to the J-B tables; and the new tables for P-waves were published by Herrin et al. (1968).

In 1987 the International Association of Seismology and Physics of the Earth's Interior (IASPEI) initiated a major international effort to construct new global travel-time tables for earthquake location and phase identification. As a result of this, two models were developed: IASP 91 (Kennett and Engdahl, 1991) and SP6 (Morelli and Dziewonski, 1993). The most significant differences between these new models and the older J-B travel-time model are in the upper mantle and core. The IASP 91 model has been adopted as the global reference model for International Data Centre in Vienna.

Subsequently Kennett et al. (1995) began with the best characteristics of the IASP 91 and SP 6 models, and further improved the global reference model to AK 135. The AK 135 model differs from IASP 91 only in velocity gradient for the D″ layer and in the baseline for S-wave travel times. The

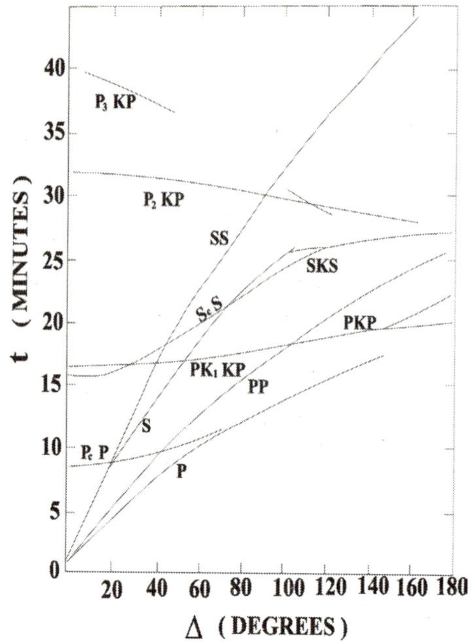

Fig. 2.41 Time-distance curves for some important seismic waves (Garland, 1979).

model AK 135, the body wave travel-time tables and plots, are available via http: // rses.anu.edu.au/seismology/ak135/intro.html, and can be downloaded and printed in postscript.

2.18 WAVE ATTENUATION

Seismic attenuation is caused by either intrinsic anelasticity or scattering effects. The intrinsic anelasticity is associated with small scale crystal dislocations, friction and movement of interstitial fluids. This effect is called *intrinsic attenuation*. The scattering effect, on the other hand, is an elastic process of redistributing wave energy by reflection, refraction and conversion that occur at discontinuities in the medium. This scattering of energy at small scale heterogeneities along travel paths reduce amplitudes of the seismic waves. These effects are called *scattering attenuation*.

The wave attenuation is usually expressed in terms of dimensionless *quality factor Q*, where

$$Q = 2\pi E/\Delta E \tag{2.42}$$

The ΔE is the dissipated energy per cycle. Large energy loss means low Q and vice versa, i.e. Q is inversely proportional to the attenuation.

We can also write an equation for amplitude as a function of distance travelled (Aki and Richards, 1980):

$$A(\chi) = A_o e^{-(f\pi/Q)\,\chi} \tag{2.43}$$

It is obvious from eq. 2.43 that for a constant value of Q a high frequency wave attenuates more rapidly than low frequency wave. Q is observed to be dependent on frequency. At higher frequency, in general, Q increases with frequency. In the Earth, Q is a function of depth, with the lowest Q values occurring in the upper mantle. In general, Q increases with *seismic impedance*, i.e. with increased material density and velocity.

The Q for P-waves in the Earth is systematically larger than Q for S-waves and thus refer to corresponding Q_p and Q_s respectively; $Q_p \simeq 9/4\ Q_s$. Table 2.5 gives approximate values of Q for different rocks.

Table 2.5: Q for different rock types

Rock Type	Q_p	Q_s
Shale	30	10
Sandstone	58	30
Granite	250	70-150
Peridotite	1200	520
Outer Core	8000	0

The mechanisms of intrinsic attenuation are very sensitive to pressure and temperature. High heat flow areas have more attenuation than colder regions. A schematic distribution of Q in a subduction zone is illustrated in Fig. 2.10.

In practice, it is difficult to separate intrinsic attenuation and scattering attenuation. Particularly, local earthquake records are strongly affected by scattering for local crustal heterogeneities, and scattering Q dominates. Scattering Q is usually determined from the decay of coda waves following S_g onsets, and is accordingly called Q_c. Unlike Q defined for intrinsic attenuation, Q_c is not a measure of energy loss per cycle, but rather, a measure of energy redistribution. Q_c is thus very much path dependent, and also strongly frequency dependent. A full discussion on this topic can be found in Aki and Richards (1980).

In this context, it may be mentioned that amplitudes of S-waves are generally five times larger than those of P-waves. This follows from the far field term of Green's function when modeling earthquake shear sources taking into account $V_p \simeq \sqrt{3}\ V_s$. Also, the periods of S-waves are longer, at least by a factor of $\sqrt{3}$, than those of P-waves due to differences in wave propagation velocity.

2.19 SEISMIC DIFFRACTION

Seismic diffraction is defined as the transmission of energy by non- geometric ray paths. In optics, the classic example of diffraction is light "leaking" around the edge of an opaque screen. In seismology, diffraction occurs whenever the radius of curvature of a reflecting interface is less than a few wavelengths of the propagating wave. Figure 2.42a shows a plane wave incident upon an opaque (acoustic impedance is infinite) boundary. Ray theory requires that waves arriving at seismometers at points *F* and *G* have identical amplitudes; no energy is transmitted to the right of point *G*. In fact, the edge of the boundary acts like a secondary source (Huygens' principle) and radiates energy forward in all directions.

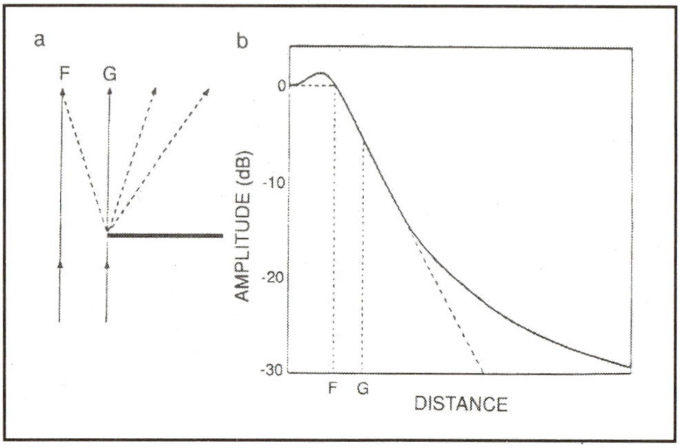

Fig. 2.42 (a) Rays incident on a grating, energy get diffracted around the edge. (b) Amplitude of energy as a function of distance into the diffraction zone (Doorbos, 1989).

These diffractions can be understood from the standpoint of *Fresnel zones*, a concept that states that waves reflect from a large region rather than just a point. Thus, the Fresnel zone causes the ray travelling to *F* to "see" the edge of the reflector, although the geometric ray path clearly misses the boundary. The first Fresnel zone may be thought to as a cone with the edge of the reflector as its apex. For a receiver, that is at a distance *d* beyond the reflector, the cone's radius is given by:

$$r = d + \frac{1}{2}\lambda \tag{2.42}$$

where λ is the wavelength of the seismic wave. Figure 2.42b shows the amplitude variation predicted for the experiment given in Fig. 2.42a.

The real Earth significantly deviate from simplified global one-dimensional models, thus scattering and diffraction affect not only amplitudes but also travel times. This has to be taken into account in recent development of automated travel-time measurement techniques. Marquering et al. (1999) showed that for an SS wave observed at an epicentral distance of 80°, near surface heterogeneities can influence upon the SS wave travel time.

APPENDIX 2.1

Modified Mercalli (MM) Intensity Scale (1956 version) (Richter, 1958)

Intensity Description

I. Not felt. Marginal and long-period effects of large earthquakes.

II. Felt by persons at rest, on upper floors, or favourably placed.

III. Felt indoors. Hanging objects swing. Vibration like passing of light trucks. Duration estimated. May not be recognized as an earthquake.

IV. Hanging objects swing. Vibration like passing of heavy trucks; or sensation of a jolt like a heavy ball striking the walls. Standing cars rock. Windows, dishes, doors rattle. Glasses clink. Crockery clashes. In the upper range of IV, wooden walls and frame creak.

V. Felt outdoors; direction estimated. Sleepers wakened. Liquids disturbed, some spilled. Small unstable objects displaced or upset. Doors swing, close, open. Shutters, pictures move. Pendulum clocks stop, start, change rate.

VI. Felt by all. Many frightened and run outdoors. Persons walk unsteadily. Windows, dishes, glassware broken. Knick-knacks, books, etc. off shelves. Pictures off walls. Furniture moved or overturned. Weak plaster and masonry *D* cracked. Small bells ring (church, school). Trees, bushes shaken visibly, or heard to rustle.

VII. Difficult to stand. Noticed by drivers. Hanging objects quiver. Furniture broken. Damage to masonry *D*, including cracks. Weak chimneys broken at roof line. Fall of plaster, loose bricks, stones, tiles, cornices also unbraced parapets and architectural ornaments. Some cracks in masonry *C*. Waves on ponds, water turbid with mud. Small slides and caving in along sand or gravel banks. Large bells ring. Concrete irrigation ditches damaged.

VIII. Steering of cars affected. Damaged to masonry *C*; partial collapse. Some damage to masonry *B*; none to masonry *A*. Fall of stucco and some masonry walls. Twisting, fall of chimneys, factory stacks, monuments, towers, elevated tanks. Frame houses moved on foundations if not bolted down; loose panel walls thrown out. Decayed piling broken off. Branches broken from trees. Changes in flow or temperature of springs and wells. Cracks in wet ground and on steep slopes.

IX. General panic. Masonry *D* destroyed; masonry *C* heavily damaged, sometimes with complete collapse; masonry *B* seriously damaged. General damage to foundations. Frame structures, if not bolted, shifted off foundations. Frames racked. Serious damage to reservoirs. Underground pipes broken. Conspicuous cracks in ground. In alluviated areas sand and mud ejected, earthquake fountains, sand craters.

X. Most masonry and frame structures destroyed with their foundations. Some well-built wooden structures and bridges destroyed. Serious damage to dams, dykes, embankments. Large landslides. Water thrown on banks of canals, rivers, lakes, etc. Sand and mud shifted horizontally on beaches and flat land. Rails bent slightly.

XI. Rails bent greatly. Underground pipelines completely out of service.

XII. Damage nearly total. Large rock masses displaced. Lines of sight and level distorted. Objects thrown into the air.

Masonry A, B, C, D. To avoid ambiguity of language, the quality of masonry, brick or otherwise, is specified by the following lettering.

Masonry A. Good workmanship, mortar, and design; reinforced, especially laterally, and bound together by using steel, concrete, etc.; designed to resist lateral forces.

Masonry B. Good workmanship and mortar, reinforced, but not designed in detail to resist lateral forces.

Masonry C. Ordinary workmanship and mortar; no extreme weaknesses like failing to tie in at corners, but neither reinforced nor designed against horizontal forces.

Masonry D. Weak materials, such as adobe; poor mortar; low standards of workmanship; weak horizontally.

3

Microearthquake Recording and Data Analysis

Introduction

Since 1980s the Geological Survey of India (GSI) has taken a lead in microearthquake investigation for detailed seismotectonics and active fault studies in various parts of India. Although this work also had important beginnings at the NGRI (National Geophysical Research Institute), IMD (India Meteorological Department), University of Roorkee (presently Indian Institute of Technology, Roorkee), WIHG (Wadia Institute of Himalayan Geology) and at the other national research institutes and universities, the work has been pursued most vigorously by the GSI in different parts of the Himalaya, Northeast India, Andaman Islands and Peninsular shield area in the country.

Choice of the seismic system for microearthquake network is a critical issue. The choice must depend on the primary uses of data. As mentioned earlier, a *temporary network* is suitable for quick data collection for seismological mapping or aftershock investigation, whereas a *permanent network* is designed for continuous monitoring of seismicity. Before we discuss on networks, we would first try to understand the earthquake recording instruments, which are called *seismographs*. The seismographs essentially have two components: *seismometer* and recorder. A recorder is an instrument which gives record of the ground displacement or velocity. The records can be analog or digital. The records are called *seismogram*. The part of the seismograph, which is sensing the ground motion, is called the seismometer. It picks up seismic vibrations of the ground and converts them into signals that can be recorded in one of a number of alternative ways.

3.1 SEISMOMETERS: THEORY AND PRACTICE

Commonly we are so much involved in analysing the seismograms and understanding the generating process of the earthquakes, that we do not give much importance on the seismometers. We do not realise on what shaky ground the seismometers are, and they don't do what the manufacturers claim they do. So, it is important that we first understand what a seismometer is, and what it can do, and what it can't do.

The motion of the ground due to an earthquake will have components in all the three cardinal directions. Usually different designs of seismometers are used for picking up different components of ground motion. Further, one group of seismologists is interested to record high frequencies, as high as 100 Hz, while another group expect to record signals with period as low as 100 second down to the prevailing noise level. More recently there is an effort with very sophisticated *long period* instruments, which record with very high *dynamic range* to bridge this gap. Their benefit to *short period* seismology is, however, questionable. Again, the amplitude of ground motion may vary over a wide range of values. This calls for different designs of seismometers, for example, for recording *strong motions* caused by a nearby earthquake, or for recording the motions due to distant earthquakes.

3.1.1 Development of Seismometers

The first known attempts to simply record the occurrence of ground motion were conducted by the Chinese. Figure 2.11 is a picture of the first Chinese seismologist, Chang Heng, and a vertical mechanical seismoscope, which he built as early as 320 A.D. It was one of the first instruments designed specially to record the occurrence of ground motion, but does not produce recording as a function of time. Significant further development of ground-motion sensors was not persued until the 1700s. The Italians developed numerous seismoscopes in the early eighteenth century. The first true seismograph, which recorded the relative motion of a pendulum and the Earth as a function of time, was built by Filippo Cecchi in Italy in 1875. The oldest known seismic record produced by this system is dated February 1887. A group of British seismologists, the best known being John Milne, James Ewing and Thomas Gray, developed first vertical component and first relatively long period systems. By 1900, the first global array of 40 photographically recording seismographs provided initial seismogram data-base to begin to understand the Earth vibrations.

Mechanical System

The principle of a mechanical sesimograph is shown in Fig. 3.1. Here a heavy mass M is hanging through a spring from a rod S, which is fixed to the ground. A pen P is attached to the downward portion of the mass M. A

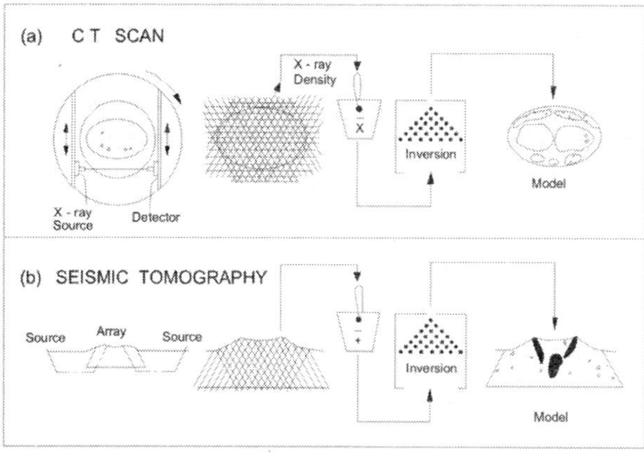

Fig. 3.40 Schematic diagram illustrating the differences between (a) medical tomography, and (b) seismic tomography (Iyer and Hirahara, 1992).

During the early years of the development of seismic tomography, the technique was called *simultaneous inversion*. The idea was to get some information on the velocity structure of the Earth, and at the same time source parameters of the earthquakes were to be determined. In the mid-1970s, it occurred to a number of seismologists that since a seismic network may have hundreds of stations, and since only four stations are required to do a hypocentre inversion, all that extra information might be put to use to invert for the velocity structure of the Earth simultaneously with the hypocentre inversion. Crosson (1976 a, b) worked out the problem for the one-dimensional case, and Aki and Lee (1976) published the results of a three-dimensional inversion. At about the same time, Aki et al. (1977) worked out the three-dimensional inversion method for velocity parameters using teleseismic events.

Examples of seismic tomography geometries are shown in Fig. 3.41, which illustrates application of local and teleseismic earthquakes recorded by an array of surface sensors. While it is possible to locate the events with a one-dimensional velocity model, the crossing-ray coverage allows us to solve for shallow crustal heterogeneity as well. The problem can be formulated for a simultaneous solution of velocity structure and earthquake locations, using the simultaneous inversion technique.

Seismic tomography is not limited to imaging the Earth or part of the Earth using body-wave arrival-time data; it has been extended to include surface waves and waveforms as well (e.g., Geller, 1991; Iyer and Hirahara, 1992). Although inverting for the Earth's velocity structure is most common, other parameters can also be imaged. For example, spatial variations in seismic attenuation from observed S to P wave amplitude ratios was studied by Ho-Liu et al. (1988), and slip velocity by tomographic source imaging of small earthquakes was carried out by Frankel et al. (1986).

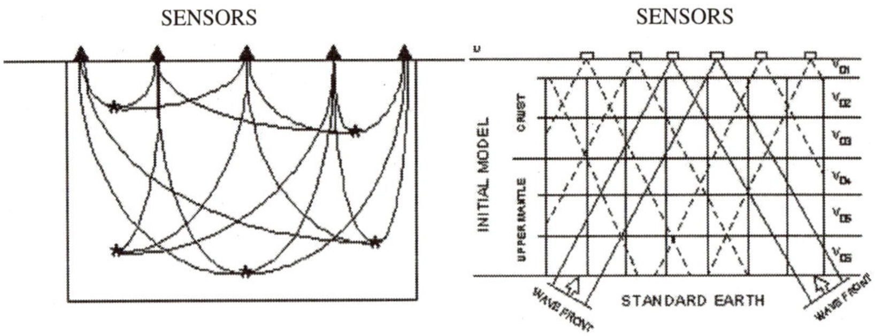

(a) (b)

Fig. 3.41 Raypaths for (a) local earthquakes, and (b) for teleseismic earthquakes (Iyer and Hirahara, 1992).

The theoretical aspect of seismic tomography is discussed by many authors (Iyer and Hirahara, 1992; Lee, 1993; Lay and Wallace, 1995). A particular seismic phase with a travel time T is represented by a path integral through the medium as

$$T = \int_S \frac{ds}{v(s)} = \int_S u(s)ds \tag{3.23}$$

where $u(s)$ is the slowness $[1/v(s)]$ along the path. The *travel-time residual* relative to the reference Earth model may be caused by a velocity or slowness perturbation anywhere along the path. A change in velocity along the ray must perturb the ray path. The path integral through the medium perturbations should equal the observed travel-time residual:

$$\int_s \Delta u(s)\ ds = \Delta T = T_{\text{obs}} - T_{\text{com}} \tag{3.24}$$

where $\Delta u(s)$ is the slowness perturbation to be determined. If the medium is subdivided into blocks, we can calculate the path length l_j in the jth block and discretize (3.24) to give

$$\Delta T = \sum_j l_j \Delta u_j \tag{3.25}$$

Obviously, a single observation is inadequate for partitioning the slowness perturbations along the path. However, if there are many event-station pairs, each with the ith ray path, we can develop a system of **i** equations

$$\Delta T = \sum_j l_{ij} \Delta u_j \tag{3.26}$$

The equation (3.26) is in the form of a linear system, which can be solved by the *matrix inversion methods*. In this case, the path length of each ray in a block, l_{ij}, is the partial derivative $\partial T_i/\partial u_j$ of the travel time with respect to the slowness of that block. The generalized inverse solution of (3.26) is provided by

$$\mathbf{m} = [\mathbf{G}^T\ \mathbf{G}]^{-1}\ \mathbf{G}^T\ \mathbf{d} \tag{3.27}$$

where $\mathbf{d} = \Delta T_i$, $\mathbf{G} = l_{ij}$, and $\mathbf{m} = \Delta u_j$. If the generalized inversion is unstable, we resort to damping or singular-value truncation to obtain a solution. The resolution matrix can be computed to reveal how well the model can be reconstructed if the data and model parameterization are perfect. Usually the resolution matrix reveals streaking between adjacent blocks where the ray coverage is inadequate to isolate the anomaly uniquely in each block.

A system like Eq. (3.27) is determined by calculating ray path segments through the model, and this is solved by *damped-least-squares, singular-value decomposition* (SVD), or by iterative procedures called *back projection* that iteratively solve the matrix equations without having to invert huge matrices.

The above mathematical techniques became popular in the 1980s as increasingly large data sets and model parameterizations were adopted. One scheme involves solution of (3.27) in the least squares form:

$$\mathbf{G}^{\mathrm{T}}\ \mathbf{G}(\mathrm{m}) = \mathbf{G}^{\mathrm{T}}\ \mathbf{d} \tag{3.28}$$

Rather than solving for the generalized inverse of $\mathbf{G}^{\mathrm{T}}\ \mathbf{G}$, one can simply use the diagonal of this matrix to approximate the solution, giving

$$\Delta u_j = -\frac{\sum_i \Delta t_i l_{ij}}{\sum_i l^2_{ij}} \tag{3.29}$$

The two sums are computed separately and updated ray by ray. Then each slowness perturbation is calculated, and the model is perturbed. In a procedure called *Simultaneous Iterative Reconstruction Technique* (SIRT), this new model is used to compute new residuals, and the procedure repeats for many iterations. Because no large matrix inversions are performed, huge models can be examined but at the cost of not computing any resolution matrices. This iterative back-projection approach was developed in medical imaging tomography (Swindell and Barrett, 1977).

Simultaneous Inversion

In the following discussion, we will concentrate on only one-type of seismic tomography, the simultaneous inversion of earthquake hypocentral parameters and velocity structure from local earthquakes. This approach is commonly used in seismology, and the basic idea can be extended for inverting for other parameters.

The simultaneous inversion problem can be posed in the following manner. There is an array of (m) stations indexed $k = 1, 2, \ldots, m$. The array is used to record (n) earthquakes indexed $j = 1, 2, \ldots, n$. The hypocentre parameters for the jth earthquake are $(t_j^0, x_j^0, y_j^0, z_j^0)$. There are n earthquakes, so the complete set of hypocentre parameters is $(t_1^0, x_1^0, y_1^0, z_1^0, t_2^0, x_2^0, y_2^0, z_2^0, \ldots, t_n^0, x_n^0, y_n^0, z_n^0)$. There are a total of $4n$ unknown parameters in this vector.

To parameterize the velocity structure, we superimpose a three-dimensional grid on the region of the crust containing the earthquake sources and the seismic stations. Figure 3.42 shows a schematic sketch of the system. Each of the cells within the grid system is assumed to have constant velocity but the velocity can vary from cell to cell. In practice, the dimensions of each block can be different. For example, around a fault, we probably want to have a finer grid than at great distance from the fault. However, for the purposes of this discussion, let us assume the cells are all equi-dimensional. Further, we assume that there are (L) blocks indexed l =1, 2,..., L. The velocity parameters of the problem are indexed (v_1, v_2,..., v_L). The complete set of unknown for the problem consists of the set of hypocentre parameters and the set of velocities, so the total number of unknowns for the problem is $4n + L$. Mathematical consideration of the simultaneous inversion given by Lee and Pereyra (1993) is briefly presented here.

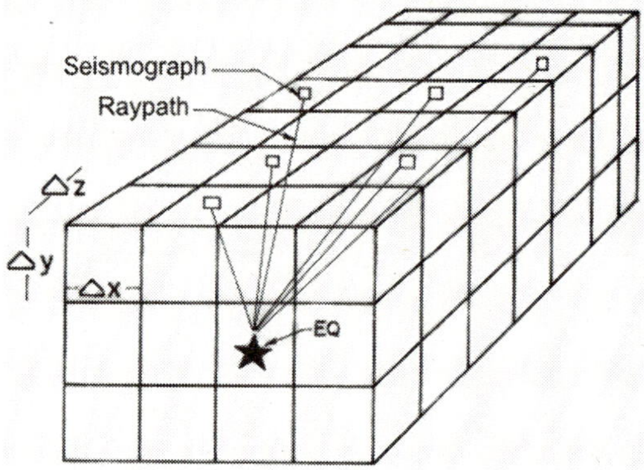

Fig. 3.42 Schematic diagram showing 3-D ray-tracing grid.

It is mathematically convenient to put all the unknowns in one parameter vector, which can be expressed as:

$$\zeta = (t_1^0, x_1^0, y_1^0, z_1^0, \ldots, t_n^0, x_n^0, y_n^0, z_n^0, v_1^0, \ldots v_L^0)^T \tag{3.30}$$

We need to define a trial parameter vector, which will be given as:

$$\zeta^* = (t_1^*, x_1^*, y_1^*, z_1^*, \ldots, t_n^*, x_n^*, y_n^*, z_n^*, v_1^*, \ldots v_L^*)^T \tag{3.31}$$

The trial vector is essentially a guess, which will be improved during the solution process. For any trial vector, the residual associated with the jth earthquake at the kth station is:

$$\mathbf{r}_{jk}(\zeta^*) = \mathbf{T}_{jk} - \mathbf{T}_{jk}(\zeta^*) - \mathbf{t}^*_j \tag{3.32}$$

Here $\mathbf{T}_{jk}$ is the measured arrival time for the jth earthquake at the kth station. $\mathbf{T}_{jk}(\zeta^*)$ is the theoretical travel time, and $\mathbf{t}^*_j$ is the theoretical origin time. There are (mn) of these residuals and in order to have a solution, we must have (mn) much larger than $(4n+L)$. Given these conditions, the problem is to minimize:

$$F(\zeta^*) = \sum_{j=1}^{n} \sum_{k=1}^{m} \left[r_{jk}(\zeta^*)\right]^2 \tag{3.33}$$

Equation (3.33) is just the sum of the squared residuals over all the stations and all the earthquakes for (mn) observations.

This is a generalization of the earthquake location problem. In the earthquake location problem, we are given a set of m stations with m corresponding arrival times, and we want to find the "best" origin time and hypocentre location, assuming a velocity model. We make a starting guess for the desired parameters, and through an iterative procedure, we improve the guess until it meets some stopping criterion. In simultaneous inversion, we do this but we also solve for the velocity model at the same time.

Just as in the earthquake location, we define a residual vector:

$$\mathbf{r} = (r_{11}, r_{12}, \ldots, r_{1m} \;\ldots\; r_{n1}, r_{n2}, \ldots, r_{nm})^T \tag{3.34}$$

Then we define the adjustment vector:

$$\delta\zeta = (\delta t_1, \delta X_1, \delta Y_1, \delta Z_1, \ldots\; \delta t_n, \delta X_n, \delta Y_n, \delta Z_n, \delta v_1, \ldots\; \delta v_L)^T \tag{3.35}$$

At each step of the process, we must solve a set of simultaneous equations for the adjustment vector in order to improve the estimate of the parameter vector. In matrix notation, the system of equations is:

$$\mathbf{B}\,\delta\zeta = -\,\mathbf{r} \tag{3.36}$$

Here **B** is the Jacobian matrix generalized to include the n earthquakes and L velocity parameters, i.e.,

$$B = \left[\begin{array}{ccccc|c} A_1 & 0 & 0 & \cdots & 0 & \\ 0 & A_2 & 0 & \cdots & 0 & \\ \cdots & \cdots & \cdots & \cdots & \cdots & C \\ 0 & 0 & 0 & \cdots & A_n & \end{array}\right] \tag{3.37}$$

Here the **0**'s are $(m$ by $4)$ matrices with zero elements, and the $\mathbf{A}_j$'s are $(m$ by $4)$ Jacobian matrices of the form:

$$\mathbf{A}_j = -\left.\begin{pmatrix} 1 & \frac{\partial T_{j1}}{\partial x} & \frac{\partial T_{j1}}{\partial y} & \frac{\partial T_{j1}}{\partial z} \\ 1 & \frac{\partial T_{j2}}{\partial x} & \frac{\partial T_{j2}}{\partial y} & \frac{\partial T_{j2}}{\partial z} \\ . & \cdots & \cdots & \cdots \\ . & \cdots & \cdots & \cdots \\ \cdots & \cdots & \cdots & \cdots \\ 1 & \frac{\partial T_{jm}}{\partial x} & \frac{\partial T_{jm}}{\partial y} & \frac{\partial T_{jm}}{\partial z} \end{pmatrix}\right|_{\zeta^*} \tag{3.38}$$

The **C** element of matrix **B** is a (*mn* by *L*) matrix where each row of the matrix has **L** elements and describes the sampling of the velocity blocks of a particular ray path. If Γ_{jk} is the ray path connecting the $\mathbf{k}^{th}$ station to the $\mathbf{j}^{th}$ earthquake hypocentre, then the elements of the ith row $[i = K + (j - 1)m]$ of **C** are given by:

$$\mathbf{C}_{il} = -\Pi_{jkl}\left(\frac{\partial T_{jk}}{\partial v_t}\right)\Bigg|_{\zeta^*} \quad \text{for } 1 = 1, 2, ..., L \tag{3.39}$$

where Π_{jkl} is defined by

$$\Pi_{jkl} = \begin{cases} 1 \; if \; l^{th} \; block \; penetrated \\ 0 \; otherwise \end{cases} \tag{3.40}$$

It is advantageous to work with slowness rather than with the velocity, where we define the slowness in the lth block as $u_l = 1/v_l$. From this, we have:

$$\delta_{ul} = -\frac{\delta v_l}{v_l} \tag{3.41}$$

To approximate the travel time derivative with respect to velocity to first-order accuracy, we make the approximation:

$$\frac{\partial T_{jk}}{\partial u_l} = \frac{\partial T_{jkl}}{\partial u_l} \tag{3.42}$$

where T_{jkl} is the travel time for the ray Γ_{jk} in the lth block. Also, $T_{jk} = u_l S_{jkl}$, where S_{jkl} is the length of the raypath Γ_{jk} in the lth block. Assuming that the dependence of S_{jkl} on u_l is of second order,

$$\frac{\partial T_{jkl}}{\partial u_l} \simeq S_{jkl} = v_l T_{jkl} \tag{3.43}$$

Thus Equation (3.39) becomes:

$$C_{il} = \Pi_{jkl} \frac{T_{jkl}\left(\zeta^*\right)}{v_l^*} \quad \text{for } 1 = 1, 2, ..., L \tag{3.44}$$

Since each raypath samples only a small number of blocks, most elements of matrix **C** are zero. Therefore, the matrix **B** is sparse, with most of its elements being zero. Equation (3.32) is a set of (*mn*) equations written in matrix form which may be rewritten as:

$$\delta t_j + \frac{\partial T_{jk}}{\partial x}\bigg|_{\zeta^*} \delta x_j + \frac{\partial T_{jk}}{\partial Y}\bigg|_{\zeta^*} \delta y_j + \frac{\partial T_{jk}}{\partial z}\bigg|_{\zeta^*} \delta z_j - \sum_{l=1}^{L} \frac{\pi_{jkl} T_{jkl}}{V^*_l} \delta v_l = r_{jk}\left(\zeta^*\right)$$

For $K = 1, 2, \dots m$, $J = 1, 2, \dots n$ (3.45)

Equation (3.45) is a generalization of the equation used for hypocentre determination. The only difference is that the simultaneous inversion equation has the summation term, which is an approximation to the sums of partial derivatives of the travel times with respect to velocity in each block.

To summarize the solution, first we guess a trial parameter vector. Essentially, one must have some estimates of where all the earthquakes are, and have some initial approximation for the velocity. Next, we calculate the theoretical travel times and the spatial derivatives for the trial vector (all stations and all earthquakes). This information is used to construct the **B** matrix. Also, we compute the residual vector, which is essentially the difference between the observed travel times and the theoretical travel times. Then we solve a system of (n by m) linear equations. This gives the adjustment vector, which is added to the trial vector. This is repeated until the solution converges to some pre-defined limit or is terminated after a pre-defined number of iterations. The process is analogous to hypocentre location, but instead of doing it for just one earthquake, we use many earthquakes, and instead of using an assumed velocity model, we solve for that as well.

The central idea of seismic tomography is not that complicated. Yet, it took nearly two decades to develop the method to its current state. It all started with the realization that local networks provided far more data than were required to locate earthquakes. From that point, the method has been refined over the years, and now there are many mathematical variations in the implementation of simultaneous inversion algorithms. However, all of them share the essential theoretical formulation of the problem that has been outlined here.

It is not possible to cover all details of the process in this brief discussion of seismic tomography. Instead, it is attempted to give a basic understanding of how the method works. If one is interested in working with seismic tomography, there are many excellent references available, such as Lanczos (1961), Forsythe et al. (1977), and Gill et al. (1981). For readers not familiar with these mathematical topics, a careful study of the above mentioned references and texts books (e.g., Menke, 1984; Tarantola, 1987) will be of great help. A collection of classic papers on inversion of geophysical data may be found in Lines (1988).

For seismic tomography, a general review by Thurber and Aki (1987) is a good start. In addition, Claerbout (1985), Nolet (1987), Lee and Pereyra (1993) and Iyer and Hirahara (1992) treat this subject in some detail. For medical tomography, Swindell and Barrett (1977) is a good introduction. In addition, there are classic papers by Cormack (1963) and by Houndsfield (1973), and a good text book by Herman (1980).

Many authors have developed software for seismic tomography study (e.g. Aki and Lee, 1976; Thurber, 1981; Paige and Saunders, 1982; Um and Thurber, 1987). A state-of-the-art software is developed by Zhao et al. (1992). Although the conceptual approach of this software parallels that of Aki and

Lee (1976), it has many additional features: (i) It is adaptable to a velocity structure that includes several complex shaped velocity discontinuities like the Moho discontinuity, dipping slab boundary etc., and images 3-D velocity variations in the model. (ii) It uses pseudo-bending technique of Um and Thurber (1987) and Snell's law to search the fastest ray. (iii) The LSQR algorithm (Paige and Saunders, 1982) with damping regulation is used to solve the large and sparse system of observation equations, allowing a great number of data to be used to solve a large tomography problem. (iv) The nonlinear tomographic problem is solved by iteratively conducting linear inversions. In each iteration, perturbations to hypocentral parameters and velocity structure are determined simultaneously to determine the crustal and mantle structure in a region. The method has been used very successfully in Japan (Zhao et al., 1992 and 2004), in Southern California (Zhao and Kanamori, 1993 and 1995), in northeast India (Kayal and Zhao, 1998), in western India, Bhuj 2001 earthquake source area (Kayal et al., 2002b) and in many subduction and volcanic zones (Zhao and Kayal, 2000).

3.13 RECEIVER FUNCTION

Although detailed investigations of the Earth structure utilize multiple seismic recordings as discussed above, a few techniques have been developed to image crustal layering or discontinuity beneath isolated three-component stations. The most widely used method is called *receiver function analysis*. The teleseismic P waves that are incident upon the crustal section below a station produce P to S conversions at crustal boundaries as well as multiple reflections in the shallow layering. It is observed that the P to S conversion has much stronger amplitude on the longitudinal component than on the vertical component. By *deconvolving* the vertical-component signal from the longitudinal component, the obscuring effects of source function and instrument response are removed, leaving a signal composed of primarily S-wave conversions and reverberations below the station. These deconvolved horizontal components are called receiver function traces and are inverted for a model of the shear wave velocity layering in the crust.

Receiver function analysis reveals the crustal interfaces at depth, but the absolute velocities and depths of the boundaries are not well resolved. Using independent determination of the average crustal velocities provided by a surface-wave dispersion analysis can provide a better constrained model. This technique can give stable results if the layers are horizontal. In such a case the receiver function is the same for all azimuths, and the tangential component of the P-wave motion is very small. In regions of three-dimensional structure, the inversion is usually ill posed, and forward modelling of the azimuthally varying receiver functions is used to constrain the crustal and uppermost mantle structure. With the invent of the broadband instruments, the receiver function analysis has become popular in 1980s (e.g. Burdick and Langston, 1977; Owens et al., 1987; Ammon, 1991). Some work is done in this line in India (Kumar et al., 2004; Gupta et al., 2003; Rai et al., 2003). There are about 30 broadband stations in the national network running in the peninsular and extra-peninsular India; the installations started since 1996 in phases. These broadband data have been very useful for this study. In addition, several temporary networks and stand alone stations with broadband instruments are being established under the DST sponsored research projects by the NGRI in peninsular India, RRL-Jorhat in northeast India and by the WIHG in NW Himalaya for this study.

3.14 SEISMIC WAVEFORM INVERSION AND MODELLING

It is mentioned early that one of the goal of a seismologist is to understand every wiggle of a seismogram, which carry information about the source as well as of the medium through which the waves propagate. These waves contain the source effects (magnitude and source time function), the propagation effects (reflectivity, diffraction, etc. in the medium) and the seismograph response effects. Mathematically each of these effects can be modelled to match the waveform of a seismogram. Such mathematical construction of a seismogram is known as *synthetic seismogram*. There are two ways to extract the information about seismic sources and subsurface parameters from seismic data: (i) *Inversion* and (ii) *Modelling*.

In inversion, the model parameters (Earth structure/source characteristics) are updated automatically until the residuals between the *synthetic seismogram* and the *observed seismogram* are minimized. In modelling, the model parameters are changed by human interference until a model is found such that the wave fields generated from the model can be best explained by the observed data. These *waveform modelling* and *inversion method* are very comprehensive compared to travel time methods (Lay and Wallace, 1995). Waveform inversion can produce results of higher resolution than travel time inversion, because it utilizes the information contained in the seismic waveform that are the source and subsurface structures. Waveform inversion and modelling are tightly coupled because inversion requires numerical modelling of wave propagation, and modelling needs a model that is obtained from the inversion.

Theoretical Aspects

Normally for full waveform inversion, earthquake source is assumed as *double couple*. In 2D, a double couple source can be parameterized as

$$s(x, z, t_0, a, R_\theta) \tag{3.46}$$

where x and z are the horizontal and vertical positions respectively, t_0 is the origin time, a is the amplitude of the double couple force, and R_θ is the angle associated with the orientation of the double couple, the local rupture direction.

For a spatially and temporally extended earthquake, the composite source parameters correspond to a series of n double-couples:

$$s(s_1, s_2, s_3, \ldots, s_n) = s(x_1, z_1, t_{01}, a_1, R_{\theta 1}, \ldots x_2, z_2, t_{02}, a_2, R_{\theta 2} \ldots x_n, z_n, t_{0n}, a_n, R_{\theta n}) \quad (3.47)$$

As this is a discrete representation, the total energy release is the integral over the energy associated with all the grid points in the area.

A seismogram or a ground motion at a site can be represented as $u(t)$**,** i.e. amplitude as function of time. In other words, in seismic waveform modelling, $u(t)$ is represented as the resultant of effects of three basic filters (Lay and Walace, 1995):

$$u(t) = s(t) \times g(t) \times i(t) \quad (3.48)$$

where $u(t)$ is the seismogram, $s(t)$ is the signal from seismic source, $g(t)$ is the propagation filter and $i(t)$ is the seismometer response. Further, the $s(t)$ and $g(t)$ can be divided into a filter that accounts for these multiplicity of arrivals due to reflections and refractions, and a filter that accounts for the attenuation. Similarly, $s(t)$ can be divided into filters that account for source radiation and fault rupture characteristics. For a more theoretical information readers should refer to Helmberger (1983), Wallace and Helmberger (1982), Lay and Wallace (1995) and many other text books.

The linear filter theory is used in constructing synthetic seismogram; the seismogram is treated as the output of a sequence of linear effects. Figure 3.43 illustrates P-wave ground displacement and its records on SP and LP seismometers. The trapzoid shape of ground motion may be considered as output of filters that account for the effects of rupture on a finite fault plane. The ground motion is then distorted by recording characteristics of the seismometers as illustrated in Fig. 3.43.

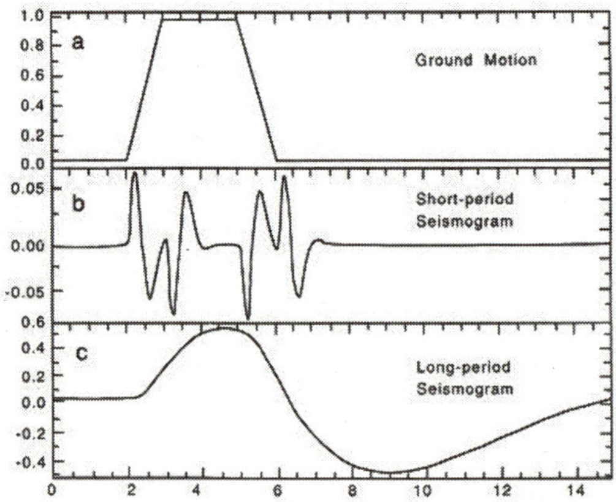

Fig. 3.43 (a) A trapezoid time function corresponding to hypothetical ground motion, (b) Seismogram produced by SP seismometer and (c) Seismogram by LP seismometer (Lay and Wallace, 1995).

For inversion we define the source region to be larger than that which we anticipate exists, and solve for the source parameters of all points in this region. In the result, only the actual source region will correspond to significant energy.

The inherently nonlinear waveform inversion is solved as a sequence of liberalized inversions. It can be represented in three directional components (vertical, radial and transverse) as below:

$$u_V(\Delta, t) = M_0 \, [a \, u_{VDD}(\Delta, t) + b \, u_{VDS}(\Delta, t) + c \, u_{VSS}(\Delta, t)] \tag{3.49}$$

$$u_R(\Delta, t) = M_0 \, [a \, u_{RDD}(\Delta, t) + b \, u_{RDS}(\Delta, t) + c \, u_{RSS}(\Delta, t)] \tag{3.50}$$

$$u_T(\Delta, t) = M_0 \, [a' \, u_{TDS}(\Delta, t) + b' \, u_{TSS}(\Delta, t)] \tag{3.51}$$

where M_0 = seismic moment = $\mu_s \, A \, D$, μ_s = modulus of rigidity at the source, A = area of the fault, D = average slip (displacement) of the rock above the fault and a, b, c, a' and b' are the coefficients and are nonlinear functions of (i) dip δ and (ii) strike direction θ of the fault, and (iii) slip direction λ of the shear dislocation constants

$$\begin{aligned} a &= \sin\lambda \sin 2\delta \\ b &= -\cos\lambda \cos\delta \cos\phi + \sin\lambda \cos 2\delta \sin\phi \\ c &= 0.5 \sin\lambda \sin 2\delta \cos 2\phi + \cos\lambda \sin\delta \sin 2\phi \end{aligned} \tag{3.52}$$

and

$$\begin{aligned} a' &= \sin\lambda \cos 2\delta \cos\phi + \cos\lambda \cos\delta \sin\phi \\ b' &= \cos\lambda \sin\delta \cos 2\phi - 0.5 \sin\lambda \sin 2\delta \sin 2\phi \end{aligned}$$

and $u(\Delta, t)$ is the response while travelling through the medium (Earth) and also depends on the type of source mechanism, time function and epicentre distance Δ. The solution for δ, θ and λ are obtained by grid search method of nonlinear inversion to get the minimum misfit error between observed and synthetic seismograms.

A general source is represented by a *moment tensor* [M] with six independent elements. However, in most tectonic earthquakes, there is no volume change at the source and thus we have only five independent elements of [M]. A synthetic seismogram is obtained by sum of five terms where each is a product of an element of [M] and the corresponding Green's function (synthetic seismogram). The moment tensor elements can be evaluated by simple linear inversion so as to get the minimum difference between synthetic and observed seismograms. The moment tensor is decomposed into best double couple moment tensor and a remaining CLVD tensor. The resulting double couple moment tensor is then interpreted for dip, strike, slip direction of the shear dislocation and percentage of double couple in the moment tensor solution.

The goal of waveform modelling is to recover seismic source parameters like source depth, time function, fault orientation and seismic moment (*moment tensor solution*) by matching the observed and synthetic waveforms. From mid 1970s through early 1980s many studies were made on the earthquake source parameters using teleseismic waveform modelling, mainly long period WWSSN data. The methodology involved matching long period P and SH waves that are well distributed in azimuth about the source (Fig. 3.44). Subsequently, attempt has been made to recover source orientation by waveform inversion at a single seismic station (Kanamori et al., 1990). Earthquakes at local and regional distances with new generation very broadband high dynamic range instruments make it possible to obtain focal mechanism for moderate size earthquakes. Source parameters can also be obtained from surface wave inversion. Surface wave inversions are best performed at long periods (>100 s). Moment tensor solutions in understanding the focal mechanism or source process are further discussed in Section 4.8.

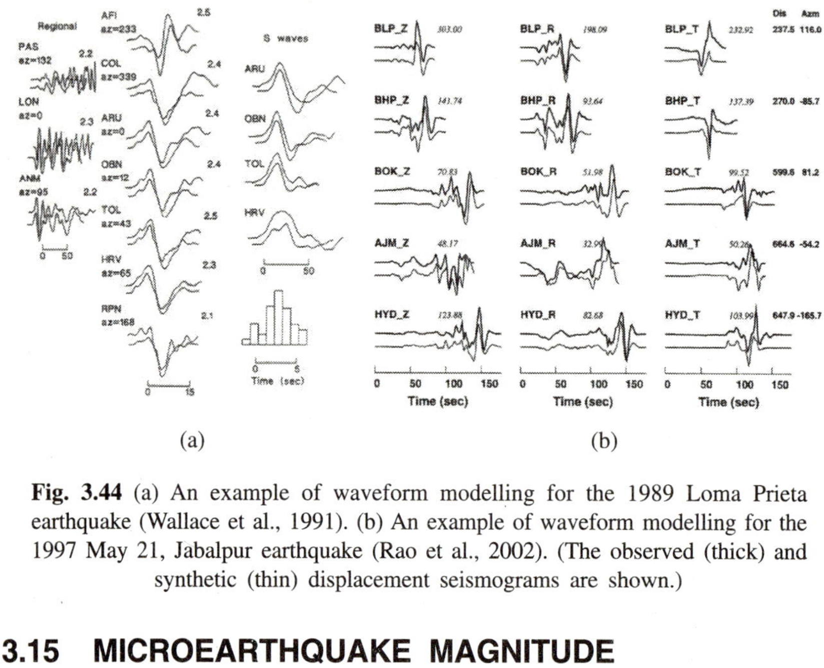

Fig. 3.44 (a) An example of waveform modelling for the 1989 Loma Prieta earthquake (Wallace et al., 1991). (b) An example of waveform modelling for the 1997 May 21, Jabalpur earthquake (Rao et al., 2002). (The observed (thick) and synthetic (thin) displacement seismograms are shown.)

3.15 MICROEARTHQUAKE MAGNITUDE

Richter magnitude scale is very popular for estimating magnitude for local earthquakes. The Richter magnitude scale is, however, based on Wood Anderson seismograph (see Section 2.1), which seldom records earthquakes with magnitude less than 3.0. So, we need a convenient method for estimating magnitude of the local earthquakes recorded by microearthquake networks with high gain instruments.

An approach was suggested by Brune and Allen (1967) to calculate the ground motion from the recorded maximum amplitude, and from this to compute the response expected from a Wood Anderson seismograph. There are, however, two problems in this approach: (i) Richter (1958) pointed out that the maximum amplitude on the Wood-Anderson record may not correspond to the wave with maximum amplitude on a different instrument's record, and (ii) maximum amplitude are mostly saturated (clipped) by the high gain microearthquake recorders.

The other approach is to use signal duration instead of maximum amplitude. This idea appears to originate from Bisztricsany (1958). He determined the relationship between earthquake magnitudes 5 to 8 and duration of the surface waves of epicentral distance 4°-160°. Solovev (1965) and Tsumura (1967) studied determination of magnitude from total signal duration for local earthquakes in Japan. Since then many authors derived empirical relationships between signal duration and magnitude for local earthquakes.

Lee et al. (1972) established an empirical formula for estimating signal duration magnitude (M_D) for the local earthquakes recorded by the USGS Central California microearthquake network using signal duration. For a set of 351 earthquakes, they computed the M_D equivalent to local magnitudes as defined by Richter (1958). Correlation of the local magnitudes with the signal durations measured by the USGS microearthquake network is shown in Fig. 3.45. They obtained the following relation:

$$M_D = -0.87 + 2.00 \log \tau + 0.0035 \Delta \qquad (3.53)$$

where M_D is duration magnitude equivalent to Richter magnitude, τ is signal duration in seconds and Δ is epicentral distance in kilometres. In an independent work, Crosson (1972) obtained a similar relation in Puget Sound region, Washington, USA.

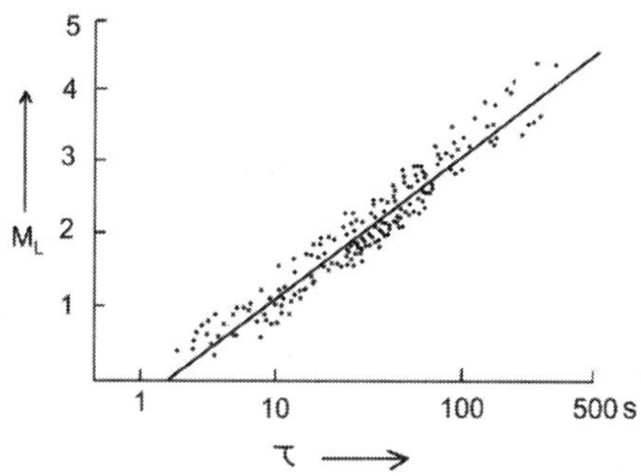

Fig. 3.45 Relation between Richter magnitude and signal duration (Lee, 1992).

Since 1972 many authors (e.g. Hori, 1973; Real and Teng, 1973; Herrmann, 1975; Bakun and Lindh, 1977; Griscom and Arabasz, 1979; Johnson, 1979; Suteau and Whitcomb, 1979) have determined signal duration magnitude and given a relation in the form:

$$M_D = a_1 + a_2 \log \tau + a_3 \Delta + a_4 h \qquad (3.54)$$

where τ is signal duration in seconds, Δ is epicentral distance in kilometres, h is focal depth in kilometres, and a_1, a_2, a_3 and a_4 are empirical constants. These constants are determined by correlating signal duration with the Richter magnitude for a selected set of earthquakes and taking epicentral distance and focal depth into account.

It is, however, important to note that different authors have defined signal duration differently. In practice, it is difficult to measure total signal duration of an earthquake. Lee et al. (1972) defined signal duration to be the time interval in seconds between the onset of the first P-wave and the point where the seismic signal, peak to peak amplitude, no longer exceeds 1 cm as it appears on a Geotech Develocorder viewer with 20 × magnification. Though this definition is arbitrary, it is easy to apply, and the measurements are reproducible by readers within 1-2 s; this much precision is fair enough to compute the M_D. Since the background noise is about 0.5 cm (peak to peak), this definition is equivalent to a cut off point where the signal amplitude is approximately twice that of the noise, an example is illustrated in Fig. 3.25. For a given earthquake, signal duration should be measured for as many stations as possible. Duration magnitude is then computed for each station, and the average of the station magnitudes is taken to be the earthquake magnitude.

Using signal duration to estimate earthquake magnitude has become a common practice in microearthquake networks. However, studies to improve estimation of magnitude of local earthquakes have been carried out. Johnson (1979) presented a method of magnitude estimation based on decay of coda amplitudes using digital seismic traces. Suteau and Whitcomb (1979) studied relationships between local magnitude, seismic moment, coda amplitude and signal duration. The signal duration relation developed by Lee et al. (1972) for estimation of magnitudes of the local earthquakes recorded by the microearthquake networks in California is, however, widely used by many authors. These estimations are found to be compatible with the Richter magnitudes.

3.16 EARTHQUAKE PHENOMENA: POWER LAW RELATIONS

The earthquake phenomena with respect to magnitude, time and space possesses *power-law* relation. The Gutenber-Richter (1944) frequency-magnitude relation, *b-value*, is a power law relation involving magnitude. Similarly *aftershock attenuation (p-value)* follows another power law, Omori Law, involving time (Omori, 1894). Two-point spatial correlation function for earthquake epicentres also displays a power law structure (Kagan and Knopoff (1980), and represents a self similar mathematical construct, the *fractal*; the scaling parameter is called the *fractal dimension* (Mandelbort, 1982). All these relations are also important to understand earthquake process and tectonics.

3.16.1 Frequency-Magnitude Relation b-value

Magnitude of an earthquake is the most commonly used parameter of earthquake size. The statistical distribution of sizes for a group of earthquakes is complicated. Gutenberg and Richter (1944) provided a simplest earthquake occurrence of frequency-magnitude relation, which describes a power law relation:

$$\log_{10} N = a - bM \qquad (3.55)$$

where N is the number of earthquakes in a group having magnitude larger than M, a is a constant and b is the slope of the log-linear relation. The estimated slope of the log-linear relation or the coefficient b is known as b-value. The b-value varies from 0.5-1.5 depending on tectonics, structural heterogeneity and stress distribution in space (Mogi, 1962; Scholtz, 1968). It has been shown that the relation also holds for aftershock sequence (Utsu 1961 and 1969).

The b-value should be estimated carefully as the self-similarity may break with the following three stages: smaller events (M<3.0), medium events ($3 \leq M \leq M_{saturate}$), and larger events ($M \geq M_{saturate}$). The smaller events may give lower b-value because of shortage of recorded smaller events, while bigger events may give higher b-value because of the saturation of the magnitude (Scholtz, 1990).

The b-values are estimated using two methods: the *least-square fit method* and the *maximum likelihood method.* In the least-square fit method, the log values of the cumulative number of earthquakes (N) are plotted with magnitude (M). A sample of plot is shown in Fig. 3.46 for the 1999 chamoli earthquake sequence. The b-value is estimated from the slope of the least square fit line, the long-linear relation of the N and M.

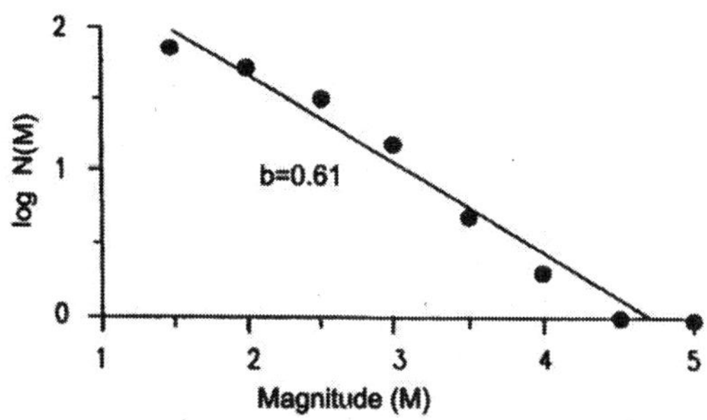

Fig. 3.46 Frequency-magnitude plot, 1999 Chamoli aftershocks, NW Himalaya (Kayal et al., 2003b).

In the maximum likelihood method, Aki (1965), based on theoretical considerations, gave an estimate of b-value as:

$$b = \frac{\log_{10} e}{\overline{M} - M_0} \tag{3.56}$$

where $\overline{M}$ is the average magnitude and M_o is the threshold magnitude. An estimate of error, standard deviation δb of the b-value was given by Aki (1965), then modified formulation was given by Shi and Bolt (1982) as follows:

$$\delta b = 2.3 b^2 \sqrt{\frac{\Sigma(M_i - \overline{M})}{n(n-1)}} \tag{3.57}$$

where M_i is the magnitude of ith event, $\overline{M}$ is the average magnitude for a set of earthquakes and n is the number of earthquakes in the set. An estimated b-value by this method for the 2001 Bhuj earthquake sequence is 1.21 ± 0.001; this is comparable with that (1.20) of the least-square fit method (Kayal et al., 2000a).

3.16.2 Aftershock Attenuation (p-value)

Omori (1894) first presented a famous formula about the time dependent attenuation of the aftershock activity, a power law relation, as follows:

$$N(t) = K/(t+c) \tag{3.58}$$

where $N(t)$ is the frequency of aftershocks per unit time interval at time t, K and c are constants.

Utsu (1957) made a modified version of the Omori's formula as:

$$N(t) \,\alpha\, t^{-p} \tag{3.59}$$

where p is a rate-constant of aftershock decay. Equation (3.59) is called modified Omori formula with exponent p =1, which implies that relaxation function for aftershock activities on frequency shows a temporal fractal property. Several researchers have empirically shown that the p-values of large earthquakes were closed to 1 but ranged from 0.6 to 2.5 (e.g. Mogi, 1962; Utsu 1969; Kisslinger and Jones, 1991; Guo and Ogata, 1995, 1997). It is, however, not clear why each aftershock sequence has a significant different p-value. Hirata (1987) argued that the p-value may be related to *fractal dimension* of pre-existing fault system in an aftershock region.

Figure 3.47a illustrates the aftershock sequence with time for the 2001 Bhuj earthquake in western peninsular of India. The aftershock frequency per day, $N(t)$ day^{-1}, is plotted against time t (days) on double logarithmic scale in Fig. 3.47b. The p-value is estimated from the slope of the regression line fitted to these data by least-square method. The estimated p-value is 0.91, near to normal p=1 (Kayal et al., 2002a).

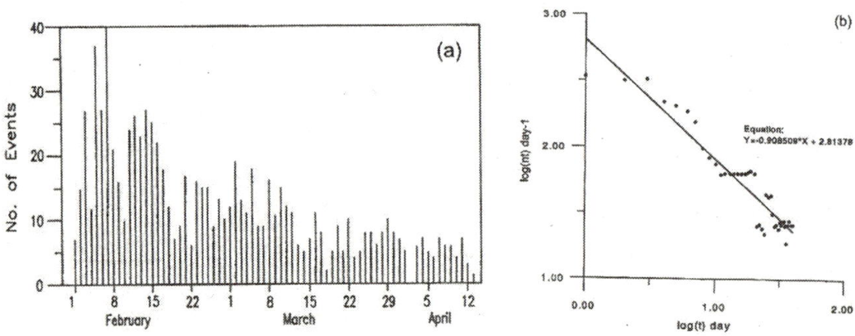

Fig. 3.47 (a) Aftershock decay with time, the January 26, 2001 Bhuj earthquake sequence, and (b) p-value of the sequence from the slope of the log-log plot (Kayal et al., 2002a).

To parameterize the velocity structure, we superimpose a three-dimensional grid on the region of the crust containing the earthquake sources and the seismic stations. Figure 3.42 shows a schematic sketch of the system. Each of the cells within the grid system is assumed to have constant velocity but the velocity can vary from cell to cell. In practice, the dimensions of each block can be different. For example, around a fault, we probably want to have a finer grid than at great distance from the fault. However, for the purposes of this discussion, let us assume the cells are all equi-dimensional. Further, we assume that there are (L) blocks indexed l =1, 2,..., L. The velocity parameters of the problem are indexed (v_1, v_2,..., v_L). The complete set of unknown for the problem consists of the set of hypocentre parameters and the set of velocities, so the total number of unknowns for the problem is $4n + L$. Mathematical consideration of the simultaneous inversion given by Lee and Pereyra (1993) is briefly presented here.

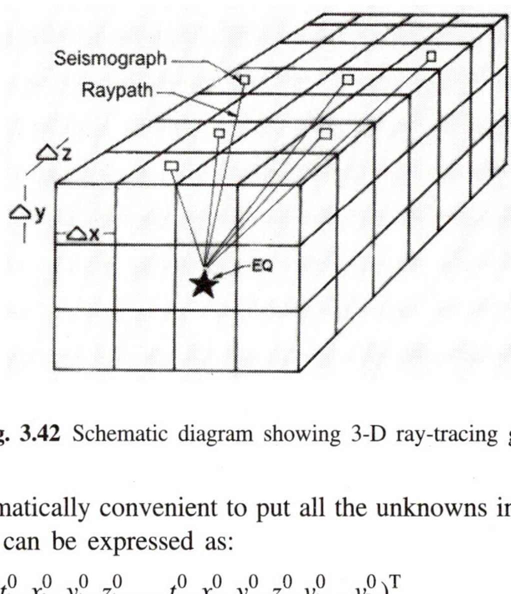

Fig. 3.42 Schematic diagram showing 3-D ray-tracing grid.

It is mathematically convenient to put all the unknowns in one parameter vector, which can be expressed as:

$$\zeta = (t_1^0, x_1^0, y_1^0, z_1^0, ..., t_n^0, x_n^0, y_n^0, z_n^0, v_1^0, ...v_L^0)^T \tag{3.30}$$

We need to define a trial parameter vector, which will be given as:

$$\zeta^* = (t_1^*, x_1^*, y_1^*, z_1^*, ..., t_n^*, x_n^*, y_n^*, z_n^*, v_1^*, ...v_L^*)^T \tag{3.31}$$

The trial vector is essentially a guess, which will be improved during the solution process. For any trial vector, the residual associated with the jth earthquake at the kth station is:

$$\mathbf{r}_{jk}(\zeta^*) = \mathbf{T}_{jk} - \mathbf{T}_{jk}(\zeta^*) - \mathbf{t}^*_j \tag{3.32}$$

Here $\mathbf{T}_{jk}$ is the measured arrival time for the jth earthquake at the kth station. $\mathbf{T}_{jk}(\zeta^*)$ is the theoretical travel time, and $\mathbf{t}^*_j$ is the theoretical origin time. There are (mn) of these residuals and in order to have a solution, we

Table 7.1: World Examples of SCR Events with Surface Rupture (Bhattacharya and Dattatrayam, 2003)

Sl. No.	*Location of Earthquake*	*Date*	*Earthquake magnitudes*	*Dominant faulting*	*Scarp length (km)*	*Max. scarp height (m)*
01	Kachchh, India	June 16, 1819	M 8.4 M_w 7.8 (revised)	Thrust (Surface fold, not a rupture; see Rajendran and Rajendran, 2001)	>90	4.3 (coseismic 5.1 (peak height))
02	Accra, Ghana	June 22, 1939	M 6.5	Sinistral ?	9-17	0.46
03	Centtral Sudan, Africa	October 9, 1966	m_b 5.1	Sinistral	6	0.00
04	Meckering, WA, Australia	October 14, 1968	M_s 6.8; m_b 6.0	Dextral>reverse	37	3.5
05	Calingiri, WA Australia	March 11, 1970	M_s 5.7; m_b 5.7	Sinistral>reverse	3	<0.4
06	Cadoux, WA Australia	June 6, 1979	m_b 6.3 Ms 6.4	Dextral>reverse	28	<1.4
07	Guinea, Africa	December 22, 1983	M_s 6.2; m_b 6.4	Dextral	9.4	0.13
08	Marryat Creek, SA, Australia	March 30, 1986	M_s 5.8; m_b 5.7	Reverse>dextral and sinistral	13	~0.9
09	Tennant Creek, NT, Australia	January 22, 1988	M_s 6.3; 6.4, 6.7; m_b 6.1, 6.1, 6.5	Reverse	32	1.8
10	Ungava, Quebec, Canada	December 25, 1989	M_s 6.3; m_b 6.2	Reverse>sinistral	10	1.8
11	Killari (Latur), India	September 29, 1993	M_s 6.4; m_b 6.3	Reverse	3	0.8

7.2 GEOLOGICAL EVOLUTION

The Indian subcontinent, covering some 3.2 million sq km in area, constitutes three major physiographic provinces: The Himalays, the Indo Gangetic Alluvial Plains (IGAP) and the Peninsular Shield.

The peninsular shield is made up of three main cratonic regions: the Aravalli, the Dharwar and the Singhbhum Protocontinents (Fig. 7.3), which are separated by 'rifts' (Burke et al., 1978). The Singhbhum block is further divided by two cratons separated by the Mahanadi graben (rift). The craton to the southwest of the Mahanadi graben is called the Bhandra craton. The Bhandra craton and the Dharwar craton are separated by the Godavari rift. The major prominent rifts, which separate the northern and southern blocks of the shield, are the Narmada Son Lineament (NSL) and the Tapti Lineament (TL), together called SONATA (Son-Narmada-Tapti Lineament) zone. It is about 1000 km long and 50 km wide (Fig. 7.2). The other prominent rift is the Kutch rift at the northwest margin of the Indian shield. The SONATA zone reactivated several times in the geological past (West, 1962); block faulting as well as horst and graben tectonics is suggested by many workers for its origin (e.g. Choubey, 1971; Roy and Bandopadhyay, 1988). There are

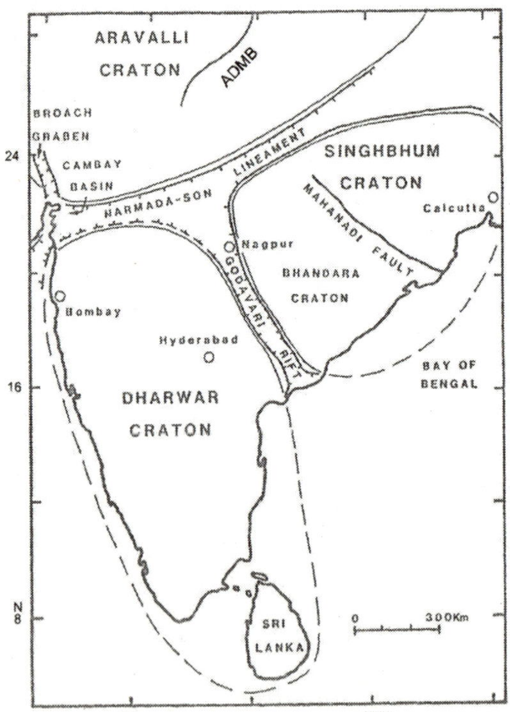

Fig. 7.3 Three main cratonic regions in peninsular India and Sri Lanka (Burke et al., 1978).

two major boundary fault systems with the NSL: a northerly dipping Narmada North Fault (NNF) and a southerly dipping Narmada South Fault (NSF) (Fig. 7.2). These are mantle reaching faults as confirmed by Deep Seismic Soundings (DSS) (Kaila, 1988) and by gravity study (Mishra, 1992; Verma and Banerjee, 1992; Agarwal et al., 1995).

The Central Core Region (CCR) of the shield area comprises granite gneisses and granites; metasedimentary and metavolcanic rocks are also associated. The SCR was cratonised before 2600 m.y. (Radhakrishna and Naqvi, 1986). The Precambrian shield witnessed broadly two orogenies falling in the time bands 2600-2000 m.y. and 2000-1600 m.y.; the first forming the early Proterozoic mobile belt and the second the middle Proterozoic mobile belt. Tectonism and dominantly acid-alkaline magmatism continued in the 1600-540 m.y. time-band, specially in parts of western Rajasthan, Kerala and in parts of eastern India (Mahadevan, 1994). The late phase of 750-540 m.y. time-band seems clearly related to a late anorogenic crustal up warping and rifting. The last tectono-magmatic episode in the peninsular shield is represented by the Deccan traps, the basaltic flows of Cretaceous-Eocene. This pile of volcanic rocks have concealed major tectonic features in the area (Fig. 7.1). Thickness of the traps is estimated to vary between 60 m and 2000 m. The Deccan traps appear to be fissure type of eruptions (West, 1958), and no large crater like structure are observed except one at Lonar lake, for explaining the eruption in terms of large volcanic eruptions. The palaeontological and geochronological data indicate that the basaltic flows become progressively younger from west to east. On the basis of K-Ar dating method, Rama (1968) reported the ages between 60-65 m.y.

The southern peninsular region constitutes three major tectonic domains; these are: Dharwar craton, Eastern Ghat mobile belt and Southern Granulite Terrain (SGT). The Dharwar craton is characterized by the Dharwar schist belt, Kolar schist belt and the N-S trending closepet granulite (Fig. 7.4). The closepet granulite belt separates the eastern Dharwar and western Dharwar blocks. To the south of this block, the Moyar-Bhavani and Palaghat shear systems separate the Dharwar craton from the SGT. The shear zones represent a transition zone marked by gradation in metamorphism from gneisses to charnokites. The gravity anomalies across this zone are smoothly varying. The SGT is further subdivided into three major blocks. The northern granulite block occupies the area between the Dharwar craton and the Palaghat-Cauvery shear zone; a transition zone between the low and high grade terrain (age ~2.5 Ga). The southern granulite block lies between the Palaghat-Cauvery shear and the Achankovil fault; it includes most of the highlands with a maximum elevation of 2600 m. To the south of Achankovil shear zone is the Kerala Khondolite block, a seat of metasedimentary granulites (2100~2830 Ma). A detailed tectonic map with aeromagnetic anomalies are discussed later (Section 7.3.2).

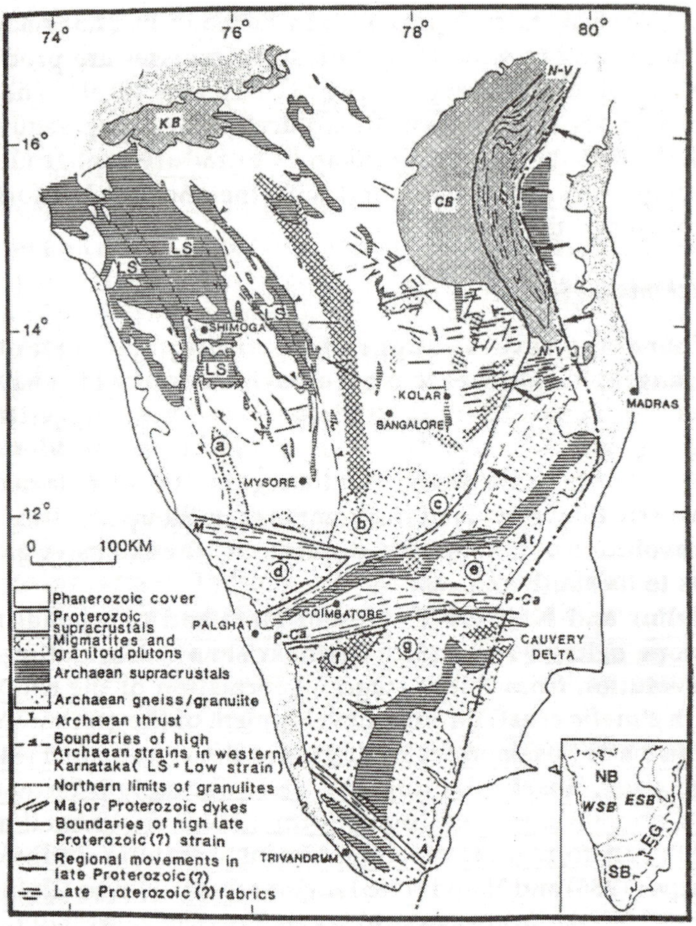

Fig. 7.4 Detailed tectonic features of southern peninsular India, CB: Cuddapah basin, KB: Kaladgi basin, N.V: Nallamalal-Velikonda, M-B: Moyar-Bhavani; At: Attur; P-Ca: Palghat-Cauvery; A. Achankovil; lower case letters a-g are granulite massifs. a-Coorg; b-Biligirirangan (B.R); c-Sheveroi; d-Nilgiri; e-Kollimalai; f-Anaimalai; g-Palni. The inset shows the main Archaean blocks in south India. EG: Eastern Ghats; NB-northern block; WSB-western sub-block; ESB-eastern sub-block; SB-southern block (Mahadevan, 1994).

The other prominent structural units are the NNW-SSE trend of the Western Ghats, NE trend of the Eastern Ghats and the major basins developed in the shield area. The major basins are discussed below.

7.2.1 Proterozoic Basins

A number of Proterozoic basins are developed mainly in the region south of the SONATA zone. These are the (i) Cuddapah, (ii) Godavari, (iii) Bhima, (iv) Kaladgi, (v) Bastar and (vi) Chattisgarh basins (Fig. 7.5). To the north of the SONATA, however, the large Vindhyan basin and smaller Gwalior basin are conspicuous. The Vindhyan basin is known to extend below the Gangetic alluvium and emerges in the Himalaya (Mahadevan, 1994). The Cuddapah, Chattisgarh, Bastar and Godavari basins to the south are regarded as middle Proterozoic. The Vidhyan, Kaladgi and Bhima are considered younger (Raha and Sastry, 1982). Krishnan (1953), however, suggested that Cuddapah, Godavari, Bastar and Chattisgarh basins possibly developed in a single basin of which they are now erosional remnants.

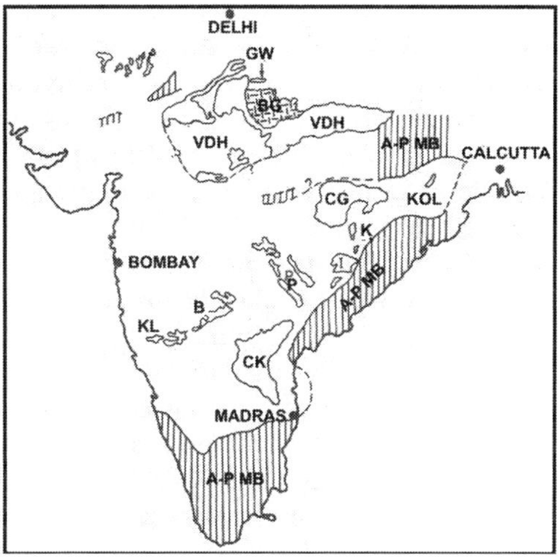

Fig. 7.5 Sketch map showing Proterozoic Basins of India; CK: Cuddapah-Karnool, P: Pakhal, B: Bhima, KL: Kaladgi, K: Khariar, CG: Chattisgarh, KOL: Kolhan, VDH: Vindhyan, BG: Bundelkhund Granite, A-P MB: Archaean-Proterozoic Mobile Belt, GW: Gwalior (Mahadevan, 1994).

All the basins to the south are largely platformal, interior fracture type basins on an ensialic crust. The basin margins have thrust contacts with the Proterozoic mobile belts. To the north, the Vindhyan basin is surrounded by the Delhi mobile belt in the west; the Great Boundary Fault (GBF) possibly separates the two (Fig. 7.2). At the southern margin, the Vindhyans are in contact with the Satpura formations and are folded. The Proterozoic sediments of the Satpura belt are reported to have been thrust over the Vindhyans (Choubey, 1971). Some details of the Cuddapah basin and the Vindhyan basin are given below.

Cuddapah Basin

The Cuddapah basin to the south of the SONATA is one of the major basins which is well studied by aeromagnetic, gravity and DSS. 2D modelling of magnetic anomalies indicate thick sediments that vary from 1.8 km to 6.5 km (Atchuta Rao et al., 1970).

The regional Bouguer anomaly map shows a gravity low of the order of -100 mGal in the basins (Fig. 7.6). There is a sharp rise in the gravity field from -100 mGal in the basin to -10 mGal over the Precambrians in the eastern side. The gravity gradient is very steep. In a detailed gravity map (Kailasam, 1976), the other major features include a rise in gravity field over Srisailam Plateau in the north and a low over Kurnool. A prominent 30 mGal rise is also mapped at Mehboob Nagar, NW of Cuddapah basin. Several attempts are made to explain these anomalies. The steep gradient of gravity anomaly along the eastern margin of the basin is attributed to ~12 km thick sediments (Kailasam, 1976), and to an intracrustal discontinuity. (Subrahmanyam and Verma, 1982). Magnetic and gravity profiles along major traverses across the Cuddapah basin indicate that the basin is made up of a number of up and down thrown blocks (Balakrishnan et al., 1967). The depth of the Mohorovičić (Moho) discontinuity estimated from a mean Bouguer anomaly map is of the order of 38 km (Fig. 7.7). Interestingly, the Moho depths estimated by the DSS profiles range from 36 to 40 km within the basin (Kaila et al., 1979). The Moho depth increases eastwardly towards the coast. The gravity modelling suggested that the Cuddapah basin could be the result of en-echelon faulting of the Moho which has an eastward down-throw leading to deepening of the basin eastward (Balakrishnan et al., 1967). A prominent reflector has been identified at a depth range 18-25 km with P-wave velocities (V_p) ranging between 6.7 and 6.9 km/s. The velocities being typical of a basaltic layer, a *Conrad discontinuity* is inferred to this reflector (Kaila et al., 1979).

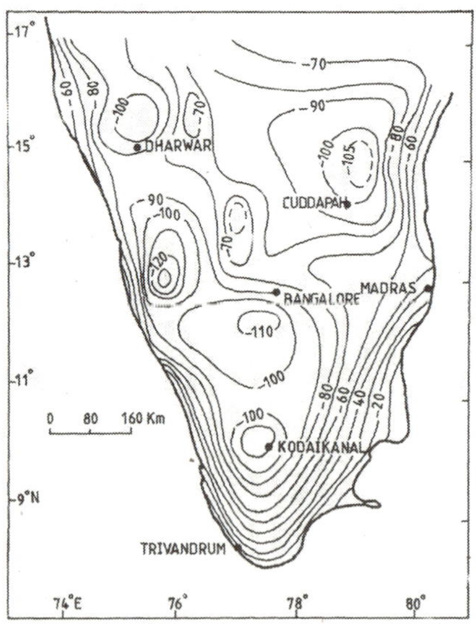

Fig. 7.6 Regional Bouguer gravity anomaly (mGal) map of south India (NGRI, 1975).

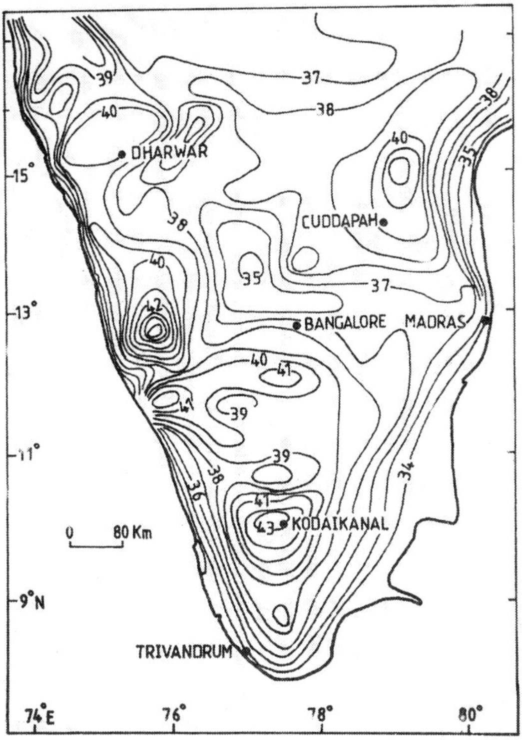

Fig. 7.7 Crustal thickness (km) map of south India, based on gravity (NGRI, 1975).

Two E-W DSS profiles across the Cuddapah basin were taken, one along (i) Kavali-Paranapalli (near 14°N), and the other along Alampur-Ganapeswaram (near south of 16°N) between 78° and 81°E (see Section 7.3.5). The DSS profiles revealed that the crust is dissected into blocks by numerous steep faults, some of which displace the Moho. The DSS results and gravity-magnetic modelling infer that the Cuddapah basin is the result of combination of factors: (i) steady dip of the Moho from west to east, (ii) thickening and thinning of the granitic and basaltic layers and the overlying sediments, and (iii) intrusion of basic magmatic material above the Moho; intrusions are exposed in the western margin but concealed at shallow depths in the eastern margin.

Vindyan Basin in the CCR

The Vindhyan basin to the north of the SONATA forms a characteristic half griddle around the Bundelkhund granite massif, covering an outcrop area of about 100,000 sq km. Some 65,000 sq km of area is under the cover of the Deccan traps (Fig. 7.1). Gravity and borehole data suggest that the Vindhyans also underlie the Indo-Gangetic alluvium (Kailasam, 1976). The real northern limits of the Vindhyan basin must possibly be in the now uplifted Lesser Himalayan region in Garhwal and Nepal. Hari Narain and Kaila (1982) suggested that the Vindhyan basin extending below the Indo-Gangetic alluvium may be divided into western and eastern parts, separated by the NE trending Faizabad Ridge, a tectonically active and growing ridge at the time of Vindhyan sedimentation. Horst and graben tectonics seem to have been prevalent resulting in a number of basement faults which led to the formation of many sub-basins. Many of these faults are active. The gravity map has been interpreted by many authors (Qureshy and Warsi, 1975; Kailasam, 1976; Mishra and Tiwari, 1981). A steep gravity gradient characterizes the western boundary of the Vindhyan basin along the Great Boundary Fault (GBF). The Archaean basement in the west thrust over the Vindhyan sediments along the GBF over a zone of 20 km wide, and a throw of the order of 6 km is estimated (Kailasam, 1976). The NE-SW trending gravity high of about 18 mGal in the centre part of the basin, supported by a positive magnetic anomaly, indicates the possible presence of basic intrusive into the Vindhyans. Spectral analysis of the Bouguer anomaly field reveals an interface, possibly the Conrad discontinuity, at about 16 km depth and the Vindhyan basement at 4.5-6.5 km depth (Mishra and Tiwari, 1981; Agarwal et al., 1995).

A DSS as well as a MT profile (Mandla-Hirapur) across the SONATA (Fig. 7.8a) that transects a part of the Vindhyan between the Bundelkhund craton exposed in the core of the Vindhyan basin in the north and Satpura formation in the south were taken (also see Section 7.3.5). It is seen that the crustal block between Narsinghgarh and Katangi forms a graben in the crystallines with ~5.5 km thick Vindhyan sediments (Fig. 7.8b). The granitic layer with Vp ~5.8 to 6.2 km/s is absent between Damoh and Katangi, the deepest part of the Vindhyan basin. The Vindhyans (Vp ~4.4-5.4 km/s) directly overlie the deeper layer (Vp ~6.0 km/s). Kaila (1988) suggested a pre-Vindhyan uplift along one of the deep faults, erosion, removal of the granitic layer and subsidence followed by Vindhyan sedimentation. Such reversals of uplift and subsidence is a characteristic of block tectonics in the SONATA belt. The MT soundings show approximately 5 km thick conductive sediments with resistivities in the range 6-30 Ωm over a resistive layer of ~200 Ωm down to a depth of 10-12 km corresponding to pre-Vindhyan crust (Fig. 7.8b).

Based on Bouguer gravity (Fig. 7.8c), Verma and Banerjee (1992) interpreted the gravity high between Jabalpur and Mandla in terms of high density in the upper crust with a density contrast of $\pm$ 0.1 gcm^{-3}. They further identified the positive Bouguer anomaly as a part of the NE-SW chain of gravity features aligned parallel to the NSL. The negative Bouguer anomaly to the north of Jabalpur is related to the Vindhyan basin sediments.

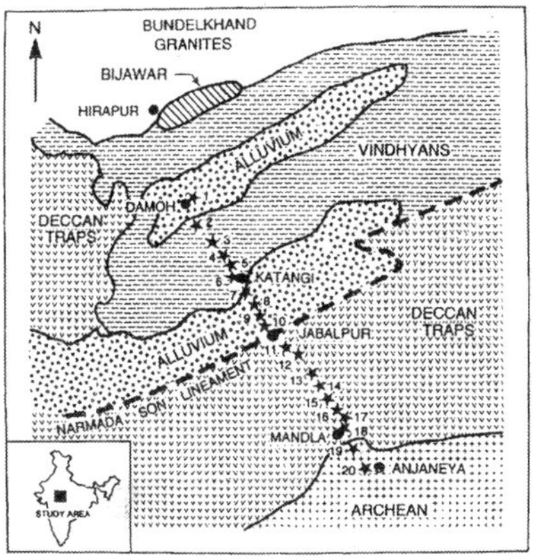

(a)

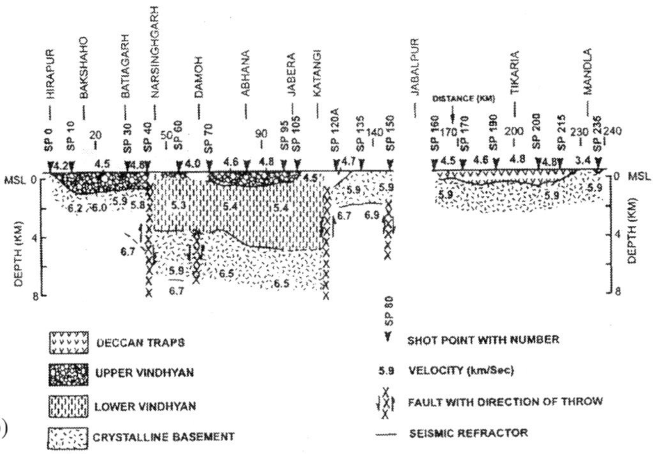

(b)

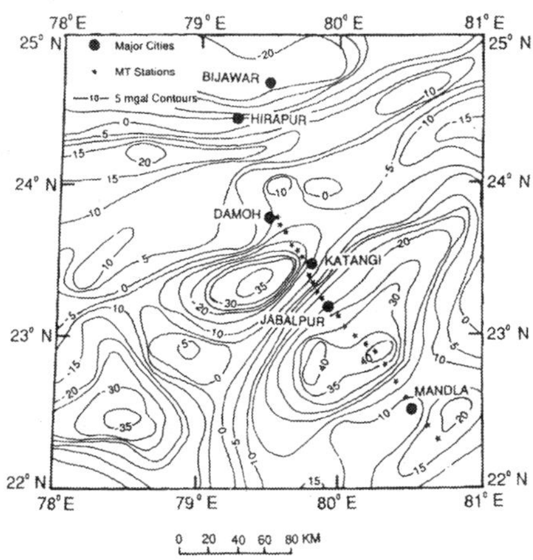

(c)

Fig. 7.8 (a) DSS and MT profiles are shown across the SONATA, from Mandla to Hirapur. (b) DSS crustal (shallow) section (Kaila et al., 1989). (c) Detailed Bouguer gravity map of the Jabalpur area (Verma and Banerjee, 1992).

7.2.2 Gondwana Basins

The Gondwana basins in India are mostly developed in major linear tectonic troughs with faulted boundaries in graben like structures. These basins are shown in Fig. 7.9. The Gondwana formations also occur as thrust sheets overlying the Siwalik and lower Tertiary formations in the Abor hills in northeastern Himalaya, and are well exposed in the Sikkim Himalaya as well.

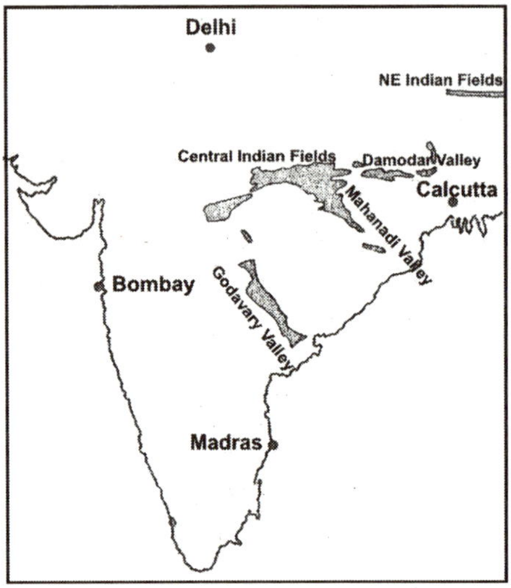

Fig. 7.9 Sketch map showing the Gondwana basins (shaded areas) in peninsular India (Mahadevan, 1994).

The Gondwanas are generally believed to have been deposited in extensive sags, which developed into grabens due to faulting contemporaneous with sedimentation. The faulted long linear belts of grabens and horsts are indicative of passive type of rifts, internal fracture basins. A Precambrian ancestry was assigned to the Godavari and Mahanadi basins (Dar and Viswanathan, 1964), and these may be the areas of merger of the Precambrian protocontinents or zones of intracontinental passive rifts (Mahadevan, 1994). Igneous activity in the Gondwana basins is rather restricted to some specific fields. Lamprophyric magmatic intrusions are observed in some parts of the Gondwana basin in eastern India, which are well recorded by borehole geophysical logs (Kayal, 1979). The dolerite/gabbro intrusions are observed in the western basins in Madhya Pradesh falling in the domains of the Mesozoic Deccan or Rajmahal igneous episodes. These intrusives are, however, not directly related to the tectonic evolution of the Gondwana basins (Mahadevan, 1994). The Godavari and Mahanadi basins are totally devoid of any igneous activity, except at Rajahmundry in the Godavari valley where Deccan traps (called Rajahmundry traps) occur on both banks of the river Godavari (Krishnan, 1960). This volcanic activity does not find expression in the lower Gondwana coal fields in the basin.

Based on gravity data, Verma and Subrahmanyam (1984) suggested that the crust is able to bear the additional load of sediments without any major readjustment. Thus there is a difference in interpretation whether the Gondwana basins are active rifts or massive interior fracture basins. Sedimentation and evolution of the basins have been controlled by block movements. The DSS profiles do corroborate with the block faulted nature of the upper crust. The crustal thickness in the Gondwana basins is not markedly different from the average crustal thickness 35-40 km for the Indian shield. There is, however, some thinning of the crust along the east coast of Mahanadi and southeast flank of Godavari, which may be due to tectonics not totally related to the graben-horst mechanisms of the Gondwana basin formation but to the later evolution of the continental margins. The Mahanadi and Godavari basins seem to end up against the Eastern Ghat mobile belt and do not extend into the coastal basins or into the Bay of Bengal.

7.2.3 Volcanic Provinces

Two major regions of Phanerozoic volcanism in India are the older Rajmahal-Sylhet Volcanic Province (RSVP) and the younger but more extensive Deccan Volcanic Province (DVP) (Fig. 7.10). The RSVP, the major Mesozoic event, is characterized by block faulting, deep crustal faults and dykes. The DVP is, however, many orders of magnitude larger than the RSVP, and it received much attention. The DVP covers some 500,000 sq km of area of peninsular India (Fig. 7.10). It is viewed as tensional tectonics and related to break up of the Gondwana land, opening of the Indian ocean and development of Arabian Sea. De Paolo et al. (1991) proposed *plume tectonics* which could emanate from differing depths, even as deep as the core-mantle thermal boundary. Dietz and Holden (1970) suggested that the Deccan volcanism manifested when the western continental margin of India passed over a thermal centre at 7° S lat and 72° E long. White and Mckenzie (1989) proposed a narrow (~150 km wide) rising plume formed by spreading out below the lithospheric plate. The model requires a steady-state long-lived plume (say ~20 m.y) beneath the slow moving lithosphere so as to generate large volume of continental basalts. These concepts are supported by many authors (e.g. Gupta and Gaur, 1984; Raval, 1989). Addressing a question whether rifting was the driving force for volcanism, Hooper (1990) suggested that primary event was the upwelling of mantle plume that caused subsequent extension, rifting and decompression.

Mahadevan (1994) classified the Deccan volcanic province into four major zones: (i) the western pericontinental Belt of Active Rift Systems (BARS), (ii) the Saurashtra Continental Block (SCB), (iii) the SONATA belt and (iv) the South East Platformal Block (SEPB).

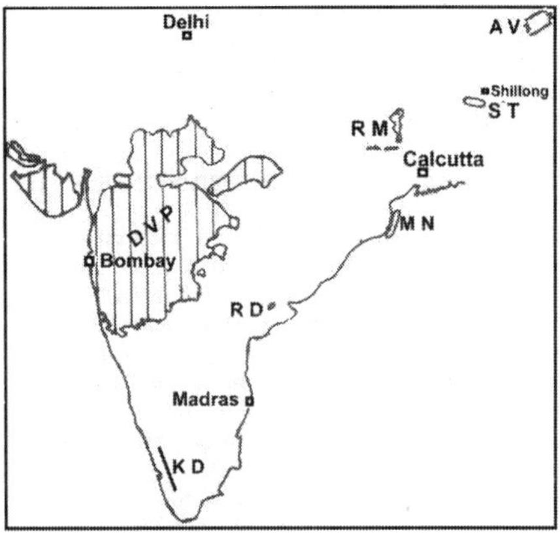

Fig. 7.10 Sketch map showing volcanic provinces of peninsular India. DVP: Deccan Volcanic Province, RM: Rajmahal and ST: Sylhet Traps, AV: Abhor Volcanism, MN: offshore Mahanadi Traps, RD: Rajahmundri Dykes, KD: Kerala Dykes (Mahadevan, 1994).

The BARS is the most dynamic of the four crustal provinces, which witnessed the most tectono-magmatic evolution in the last 60–70 m.y. It comprises the Cambay rift to the north extending southward to Bombay and offshore region. The Cambay rift has a crust thinned down to some 33 km and is characterized by 'rift cushions' of about 10 km thick. P-wave delays reveals a prominent low velocity zone at a depth range 80-200 km in the western coastal area (Iyer et al., 1989; Kennett and Widiyantoro, 1999), and the feature has been related to possible zones of magma generation in the mantle and rift system that provided channel for the Deccan volcanism.

The SCB, on the other hand, has a Precambrian thickened crust 38-43 km. It is intruded by magmatic complexes mantle lineage. The SONATA belt is characterized by ENE-WSW trending horsts and grabens, and also by thickened crust 38-45 km. The SONATA crust is highly reflective; it may be due to magmatic under plating or fluid enriched layers of the lower crust (Mahadevan, 1994). The Deccan volcanism manifests an extensive flow to the western part of the belt bordering BARS. There is lack of well developed 'rift-cushions' in the DSS profiles across the SONATA (Kaila et al., 1990).

The SEPB has normal crust of about 38 km thick. The DSS and geoelectric modelling reveals about 500 m of Deccan traps overlying the granitic basement, and the *Conrad discontinuity* at a depth of 12-18 km (Kaila et al., 1990). Teleseismic tomography reveals the presence of a high velocity (1-4% faster) layer at 100-400 km beneath most of the SEPB (Rai et al., 1992). Gravity field in the vast area of SEPB is negative, whereas it is positive in the SONATA and SCB. The positive trends are inferred to up warp of the Moho, presence of large plugs and intrusives, relative thickening of the upper granitic crust and thickening of the sedimentary supracrustals.

7.2.4 Younger Sedimentary Basins

The younger sedimentary basins of India can be classified into two groups: (i) the pericratonic sedimentary basins of Mahanadi, Godavari and Cauvery deltas along the east coast, and the Cambay basin at the western margin of the peninsular shield, (ii) the intracratonic Punjab-Rajasthan basin, the Ganga basin and the Brahmaputra-Bengal basin fringing the peninsular shield along its northern and eastern borders. The geographical locations of these basins are shown in Fig. 7.11. These basins are different in tectonic setting, but leave some common basement tectonic features, primarily one of block faulting and vertical tectonics.

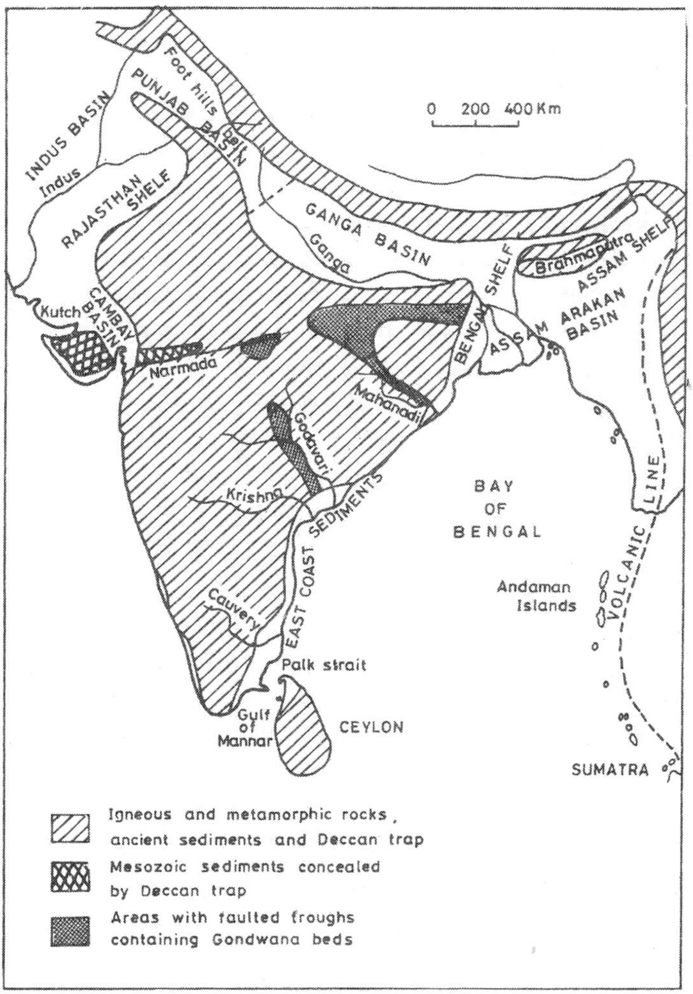

Fig. 7.11 Sketch map showing younger sedimentary basins in India, Bangladesh, Myanmar and Sri Lanka (Mathur and Evans, 1964).

All these basins are made up of horsts and grabens, and arched up basement evolved over a period of time. These are separated by many deep mantle faults with histories of more than one subsidence-sedimentation-uplift cycle. These are products largely of dilatational tectonics, the dominant Precambrian shield have participated and on which are superimposed effects of the Himalayan and coastal neotectonics (Mahadevan, 1994). The Cambay basin has all the features of an active rift and opens into the Arabean sea. The down faulted Bengal basin, on the other hand, is bounded by gravity faults in the west as well as in the north and by the Arakan Yoma anticlinal uplift, fold belts in the east. It represents a deltaic transition opening into the Bay of Bengal in the south, and is underlain by oceanic crust.

Offshore of the Mahanadi basin are basalts, which may be oceanic or representative of Rajmahal volcanics (Mahadevan, 1994). The Gondwana grabens of the Mahanadi and Godavari valleys seem to end up against the Eastern Ghat Mobile Belt, and do not extend into the coastal basins or into the Bay of Bengal. The Cauvery basin, however, occupies a layer, down faulted Precambrian central block, which may extend into the Bay of Bengal.

The Rajasthan shelf, the Indo-Gangetic Alluvial Plains (IGAP) and the upper Assam Brahmaputra valley are characterized by foredeep along the Himalayan fronts. The structure of the IGAP is debated. The structure has been projected as rift or as that of a basin. If the Himalayan major lineaments, the MCT and MBT, had a Precambrian ancestry, the IGAP may have been an early rift. Modern concept of '*skin tectonics*' or the tectonics of low angle under thrusting by intracrustal wedges require that crust below the IGAP to have a dynamic character, but in contrast, the IGAP seem to be passive, adjudged from the undeformed character of a large part of the overlying sediments (Mahadevan, 1994).

The IGAP has been commonly interpreted as a foredeep (see Section 5.6), as a rift filled with alluvium (Burrard, 1915), as a trough of steeply subducting Indian plate (Holmes, 1965) and as a basin in which the Indian shield dips at a low angle below the IGAP and under thrusts the overlying Lesser and Higher Himalayan sedimentary wedge. The basement contour map of the IGAP is presented in Fig. 5.14 (Chapter 5). The Bouguer gravity anomalies run almost parallel to the length of the basin with some prominent northeast inflections (see Fig. 5.16, Chapter 5). These northeast inflections may reflect the extension of the shield elements and subsurface ridges.

Geophysical and drilling investigations revealed many basement ridges and depressions defining the basement geometry of the IGAP in relation to the Siwalik foredeep to the north and peninsular shield to the south (see Fig. 5.15). The major subsurface ridges beneath IGAP include the Delhi-Aravalli ridge, the Faizabad ridge, the Mungher-Saharsa ridge and the Goalpara ridge. The Delhi-Aravalli horst has been redefined and expanded from the original concept of the Delhi-Hardwar ridge (Eremenko and Negi et al., 1968). Based on structural pattern and gravity observations most of these ridges are inferred to be bounded by faults.

7.3 GEOPHYSICAL FEATURES

The major geophysical inputs comprise isolated detailed studies using specific techniques like ground magnetic, aeromagnetic, gravity, DSS, magsat, magnetotelluric etc. These studies revealed the subsurface major tectonic features; a few are illustrated below.

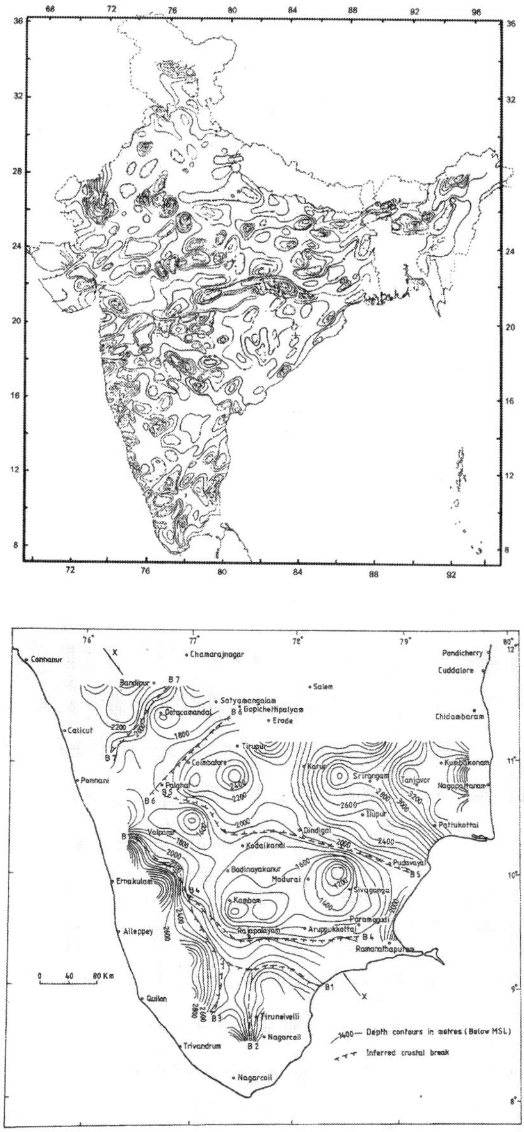

(a)

(b)

Fig. 7.12 (a) Total intensity magnetic map of India (Qureshy and Midha, 1986). (b) Base of the magnetic crust derived from Magsat data by inversion, south India (Mishra, 1986).

7.3.1 Ground Magnetic Map

Qureshy and Midha (1986) published a total intensity residual magnetic anomaly map of India based on available ground magnetic observations (Fig. 7.12a), which marks many broad features. The SONATA is clearly revealed by a prominent ENE trending magnetic feature. The NE trending Aravalli-Delhi systems also find an expression in the magnetic trends. A prominent low magnetic feature over the Mahanadi Gondwana basin continues further NW over the Deccan trap region. Qureshy and Midha (1986) infer that this magnetic feature indicates the existence of Gondwana beneath the Deccan traps. In the Indo-Gangetic plain, the magnetic contours distinguish a NW-SE trending feature in the west and an E-W trending feature in the east with a central low. There are many other strong magnetic features, which are comparable with the geologic setting of the region.

7.3.2 Aeromagnetic Map

Aeromagnetic survey is the most economical method of undertaking a geophysical reconnaissance. The aeromagnetic map provides data on broad scale structural trend, basement features and faults. A national programme was first taken up by the NGRI and then by the GSI in 1980s. Some results were published in the form of total intensity contour maps but not corrected for variations due to the main field of the Earth. Some regions were surveyed under the projects such as *Operation Hard Rock, Project Vasundhara* for mineral exploration (Reddi et al., 1988). Harikumar et al. (2000) and Rajaram et al. (2000) prepared the aeromagnetic anomaly map up to 16°N and made an attempt to interpret the anomalies in relation to deeper crust and basement features in the southern part of the peninsular shield (Fig. 7.13).

The aeromagnetic anomaly map depicts the major tectonic elements in the region with change in gradient and trend. A striking contrast in gradient is visible across the Moyar-Bhavani shear zone at ~12°N, which indicates change in magnetic sources (Fig. 7.13b). Further, looking from north to south, the predominant trends change from NW-SE to E W. Amongst two major NW-SE trending lineaments, one cuts across the Cuddapah. These features are comparable with the gravity observations (Fig. 7.6). The Wajrakarur (WK) lineament/fault is possibly responsible for the crescent shape of the Cuddapah basin (Harikumar et al., 2000). The other major NW-SE lineament to the northeastern edge of closepet granite is called Sandur lineament. The various basins such as Cauvery, Krishna-Godavari, Palar and Cuddapah are characterized by magnetic lows. In southernmost part, the NW-SE trending major feature is comparable with the Achankovil (AK) shear zone. Prominent magnetic high is observed over Khondolite to the south of AK shear zone. The Palghat-Cauvery shear zone seems to extend

aspect of this earthquake is that the source is well estimated in the lower crust at 35-40 km (Bhattacharya et al., 1997; Kayal, 2000; Singh et al., 2000), similar to the moderate earthquakes reported from the Amazona ancient rift system in SCR of South America (Zoback and Richardson, 1996). This was the first significant earthquake that was recorded by the BB stations established in peninsular India in 1996. Maximum intensity reached VIII in the MSK scale (Fig. 7.32). Fault-plane solution shows a reverse faulting with left-lateral strike-slip motion (Fig. 7.2). Details of the aftershock investigation are given in Section 7.6.

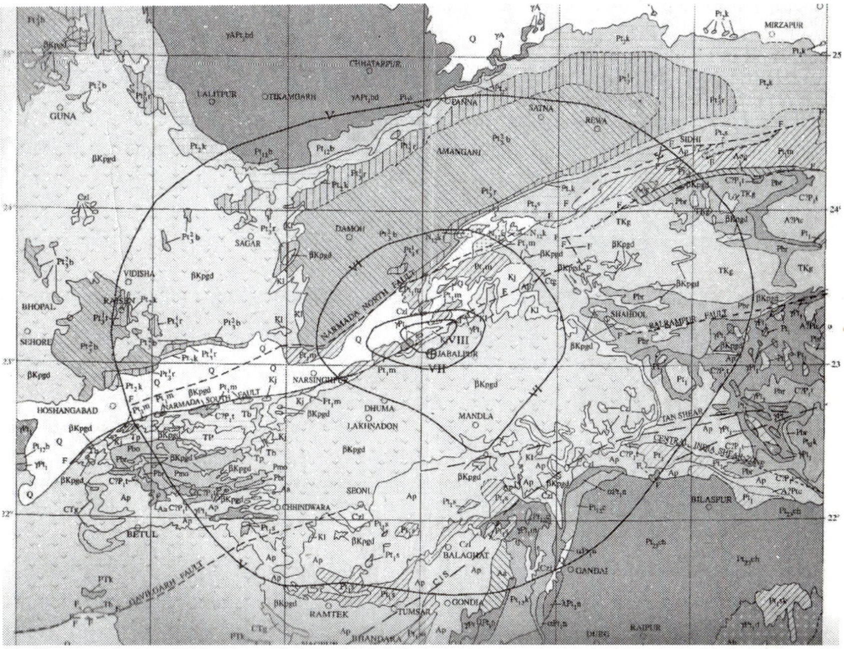

Fig. 7.32 Isoseismal map of the Jabalpur earthquake (GSI, 2000b).

7.4.5 Cambay Seismic Zone

This seismic zone is an extension of the Panvel seismic zone. Structurally this zone is related to the Cambay graben, which is terminated to the south by the Narmada North Fault (Fig.7.2). The graben is bound by the NNW striking deep normal faults. Two significant historical earthquakes occurred in this zone; one occurred on April 26, 1848 in the Mount Abu area, and the other on April 29, 1864 in the Ahmedabad area (Chandra, 1977). Both the earthquakes were well felt, and an intensity VII was assigned for both the events. A significant earthquake, magnitude 5.3, occurred in 1969 in this zone, and is known as the 1969 Mt Abu earthquake.

Mt Abu Earthquake (m_b 5.3), 1969

The October 24, 1969 earthquake, m_b 5.3, depth 15 km, epicentre at 24.8°N and 74.4°E, occurred in the Mt Abu region. Maximum intensity VII was reported. Fault plane solution of this event shows a left lateral strike slip motion (Fig. 7.2).

7.4.6 Aravalli Seismic Zone

This zone is related to the Aravalli range (Fig. 7.28). Seismic activity in this zone is small, and identification of the Aravalli range as a separate seismic zone is questionable (Chandra, 1977). It is possible that this zone extends across the Cambay graben and extension includes the Mount Abu earthquake of April 26, 1848 and the Paliyad earthquake of July 23, 1938, intensity VII. The meizoseismal trend (intensity X) of the recent 2001 Bhuj earthquake in the Kutch is also correlated with the Aravalli trend (Ravishanker and Pande, 2001).

7.4.7 Rann of Kutch Seismic Zone

The Kutch (also called Kuchchh) basin is distinguished by east-west oriented high lands (uplifts) and low lying basins or Ranns (Ranns means uninhabited salt flats that are neither sea nor land, and are flooded periodically).

The seismic zone trends northwest, and it merges with the northeast seismicity trends related to the Owen fracture zone and Kirthar range near Karachi in Pakistan (Fig. 7.28). The Chagos-Laccadive ridge intersects the coastline near this junction. A number of E-W faults control the structural trend of the Kutch Rift Basin (KRB). These are: Nagar Parkar Fault (NPF), the Allah Bund Fault (ABF), Island Belt Fault (IBF), Kutch Mainland Fault (KMF) and North Kathiwar Fault (NKF) (see Section 7.6.4). The NPF is the northern boundary and the NKF is the southern boundary faults of the KRB. The basin is filled with sediments ranging in age from middle Jurassic to Tertiary. The Deccan trap lava divides the Mesozoic and Tertiary stratigraphy of the KRB. After the initial period of extension the KRB has been subjected to N-S compression at least since 20 ma (Talwani and Gangopadhyay, 2001). The Bouguer gravity anomaly in the KRB is high and the contours also show E-W trend (GSI, 2001a). In addition to E-W faults, the basin is transected by N-S to NE-SW and NW-SE tectonic lineaments that include the structural median high (Hinge Zone) to the west of Bhuj, NE-SW Anjar-Rapar lineament, NW-SE Bhachau lineament etc. (Biswas, 1987; Talwani and Gangopadhyay, 2001; Kayal et al., 2002a).

The Kutch falls in the high seismic zone, zone V, in the seismic zoning map of India (Fig. 2.20). Among the past large earthquakes in peninsular India, the largest SCR earthquake was the 1819 Kutch earthquake (M ~8.0). This earthquake occurred before the invention of seismograph. There are several large and significant earthquakes in this zone, these are as follows:

Samaji Earthquake (intensity X), 1668

The May, 1668 earthquake, intensity X (RF scale), occurred in the Samaji area, Delta of Indus (Fig. 2.17). A report described that the Samaji town had sunk into the ground with 30,000 houses by this earthquake (Chandra, 1977).

Kutch Earthquake (M ~8.0), 1819

The Rann of Kutch earthquake of June 16, 1819, M ~8.0, intensity XI (MM scale) was felt over a large portion of Indian subcontinent, as far as Calcutta (Oldham, 1883). This was assigned to be a great earthquake in the Indian shield (Fig. 7.2). Details of this earthquake are given in Section 2.7.1. In recent studies, magnitude of this event is, however, revised to M_W 7.8 (Johnston and Kanter, 1990; Ambraseys and Douglas, 2004). The spectacular feature of this earthquake was the creation of a ~90 km long elevated tract of land called Allah Bund (Dam of God) close to the international border between India and Pakistan. Rajendran et al. (1998) suggested a low angle reverse faulting for this earthquake, and they located the epicentre to the north of Allah Bund Fault (Fig. 7.2).

Evidences for two older events have been obtained from *paleoseismological* studies in the Kutch region (Rajendran et al., 2002). Paleoliquefaction features in Dholka area near Ahmedabad, a site located within the Cambay basin, suggest evidence for occurrence of an earthquake about 3,000 yr B.P.; its source remaining uncertain. The other major event is indicated by Archeological evidence at Dholavira, a major ancient Harappan city (B.C. 2600 to BC 1600) (Joshi and Bisht, 1994).

Anjar Earthquake (M_W 6.0), 1956

The earthquake of July 21, 1956, magnitude M_w 6.0, intensity IX (MM scale), in the Anjar area caused considerable damage to a number of villages in the central mainland of Kutch. About 115 people were killed, hundreds were injured, 1,350 houses destroyed in Anjar town alone. The area of maximum damage was about 2,000 sq km. The radius of perceptibility was about 300 km. The isoseismal map is shown in Fig. 7.33. This event was fairly well studied by Chung and Gao (1995). A reverse fault-plane solution was inferred for this event (Fig. 7.2).

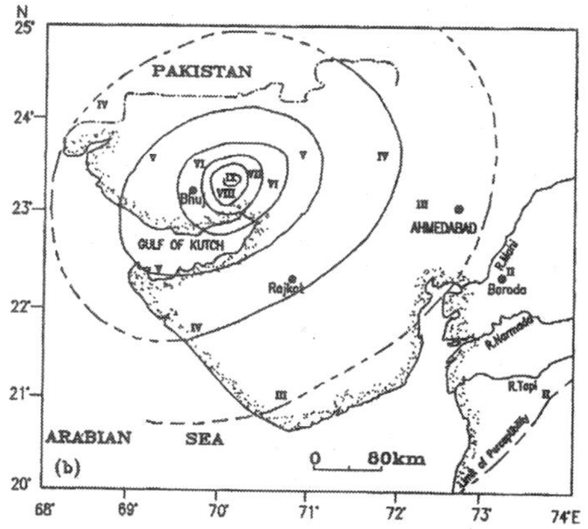

Fig. 7.33 Isoseismal map of the 1956 Anjar earthquake (M_w 6.0) (Tandon, 1956).

Bhuj Earthquake (M_w 7.7), 2001

The January 26, 2001 Bhuj earthquake (M_w 7.7) in western India is one of the most deadly and well reported intraplate earthquakes in the world (e.g. Gupta et al., 2001; Bendick et al., 2001). The moment magnitude (M_w), estimated by different organizations, ranges from 7.5 to 7.7 suggesting a rupture of 15-30 km width, 50-100 km length and average slip 4-6 m at depth. Surface manifestation of such rupture is likely to be a broad zone of distributed uplift and subsidence with secondary surface faulting and cracking (Wesnousky et al., 2001).

Macroseismic surveys were carried out by several groups of scientists immediately after the main shock, and several reports are available (e.g. Ravishanker and Pande, 2001; Rastogi, 2001a; Wesnousky et al., 2001; McCaplin and Thakkar, 2001; Rajendran et al., 2001). A detailed report is published by the Geological Survey of India (GSI, 2003). The earthquake caused a maximum intensity of X (MSK scale) in an area of 780 sq km (Fig. 7.34a). The inhabitants narrated that just before the severe ground shaking there was an explosion or deep rumbling sound, the *earthquake sound.*

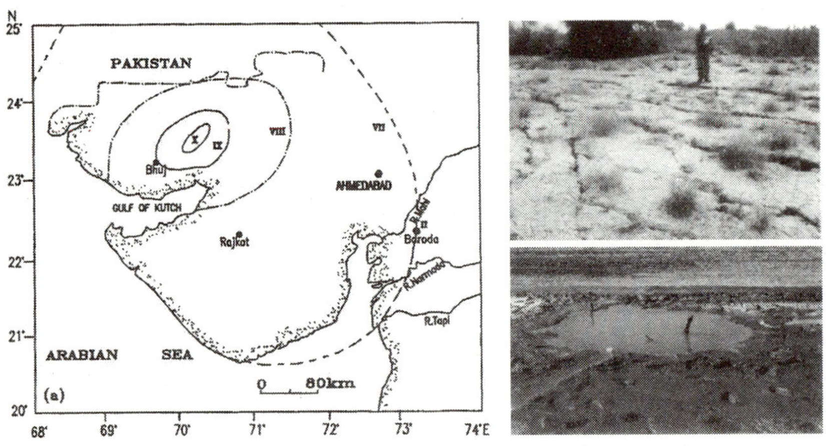

(a) (b)

Fig. 7.34 (a) Isoseismal map of the January 2006 Bhuj earthquake (Pande et al., 2003). (b) Ground cracks and liquefaction in the intensity zone VIII in Bhuj area (Rajendran et al., 2001).

Destruction of civil structures, irrespective of class or type of construction, was near total in the meizoseismal area, isoseist X. The isoseist IX comprised an area of 10,455 sq km (Ravishanker and Pande, 2001). In this zone also, many of the well built structures failed totally. No primary surface rupture was reported. Wesnousky et al. (2001), however, reported about 8 km long secondary rupture along the Bhachau lineament; they called it Manfara rupture which passes through the Manfara town; the rupture showed right lateral motion up to 32 cm of slip. They have also reported a scarp, about 50 cm high, that strikes east-west over several hundred metres. About 100 m south of the scarp, the ground was pervasively fractured by extensional cracks.

Profuse liquefaction in an area of about 50,000 sq km was reported in the form of sand blows/boils, craters, ground fissures, slumps etc. (Ravishanker and Pande, 2001; Rajendran et al., 2001). The sandy plains of Rann of Kutch and the Little Rann, where groundwater level was at shallower depths, have provided the most conducive environment for liquefaction in intensity zone VIII and above (Fig. 7.34b).

7.4.8 Girnar Seismic Zone

This zone extends into the Kathiwar peninsula, almost in line with the SONATA zone (Fig. 7.28). It is one of the four seismic zones, which were probably related to a plume generated four-armed rift junction, described as Khambat junction by Burke and Dewey (1973a). Chandra (1977) suggested that the earthquakes in this zone may be related to the Rann of Kutch zone, but existence of a fault along a direct continuation of the Narmada North fault near the Gir coast should not be ignored to assess the seismic potential of the Girnar zone. The Bhavnagar earthquake of April 21, 1919, intensity VIII, was well felt at Bhavnagar and nearby villages. The historical data indicate that a moderate earthquake (M~6.0) occurred in Surat in 1684 AD (Oldham, 1883).

7.4.9 East Coast Seismic Zone

The area consists part of Dharwar Craton and Eastern Ghat Granulite Belt (EGGB) separated by a prominent shear zone (Fig. 7.28). The principal structural trend is approximately N-S; the region is traversed by fairly dense network of medium and mega lineaments. Gravity trends conform fairly well with the structural trend. E-W gravity trend is observed over the Dharwar craton with values decreasing towards north. The gravity value decreases to –110 mGal near the centre of the Cuddapah basin where the sediment thickness is maximum. The EGGB is marked by N-S gravity trend (Fig. 7.15). A significant earthquake is reported in this zone as given below.

Ongole Earthquake (M 5.4), 1967

The March 27, 1967 Ongole earthquake (m_b 5.4), depth 17 km, epicentre at 15.6°N and 80.1°E, occurred on the NNW-SSE trending Gundlakumma fault traversing the Nellore schist belt. Right lateral strike-slip solution is inferred for this event (Fig. 7.2).

7.4.10 Godavari Valley Zone

The Godavari valley is a Mesozoic rift with a length of ~800 km, that separates the Dharwar craton to the west and the Bhandara craton to the east, and represents a polycyclic structural trend in NNW-SSE direction (Fig. 7.2). The eastern margin of the Godavari rift is bound by NNW-SSE trending basin margin fault. Bouguer gravity anomaly displays conformity with the tectonic domain (Fig. 7.15). The gravity over the graben shows a steep gradient; it drops from 30 mGal at the basin margin to around -100 mGal with low amplitude circular patterns at the centre of the basin where the sediment thickness is maximum. Two DSS profiles across the valley reveals the presence of two sedimentary basins (Kaila et al., 1990); the Godavari graben and the Godavari coastal basin, separated by a basement ridge. It has also indicated the presence of 2.8 km thick lower Gondwana sediments within the graben.

Historical records indicate not many significant earthquakes occurred in the Godavari valley region during the last two hundred years, only a few minor events were reported (Gupta et al., 1970). Seismicity is mostly confined to the Godavari basin, towards southeastern end in the Bhadrachalam area, where a significant event (m_b 5.3) occurred in 1969.

Bhadrachalam Earthquake (m_b 5.3), 1969

On April 13, 1969, the strongest earthquake m_b 5.3, M_S 5.7, occurred in the Godavari valley region, that shook the entire Andhra Pradesh at 8.56 pm (IST). The ISC located the epicentre at 17.9°N and 80.6°E near Bhadrachalam, with an origin time 15h 24m 55.7s (GMT). The focal depth was estimated at 17 km. The maximum intensity VII (MM scale) was reported for this event (Fig. 7.35). The main shock was preceded by a few foreshocks. The aftershocks were confined to a shallow depth 10-15 km within a narrow zone of 10 × 20 sq km (Gupta et al., 1970), which indicate that the main shock was at a shallower depth. The b-value of the sequence was estimated to be 0.51, typical of shield seismicity. Focal mechanism of the main shock was reported by several authors (Fig. 7.35). Chandra (1977), using WWSSN P-wave first motion data, gave two solutions; one strike-slip solution and the other pure reverse faulting, and it was not clear which one is right (a and b, Fig. 7.35). Chung (1993) did waveform modelling of the P and SH waves recorded by the WWSSN, and gave a fault plane solution (c, Fig. 7.35), which is consistent with the strike slip solution (a) of Chandra (1977). The NE-SW nodal plane is conformable with the meizoseismal trend, as well as with the aftershock trend, and it was inferred that the NE-SW trending conjugate fault of the Godavari valley was the seismogenic fault. Estimated stress drop was $\Delta\sigma$ = 16.88 bar (Chung, 1993).

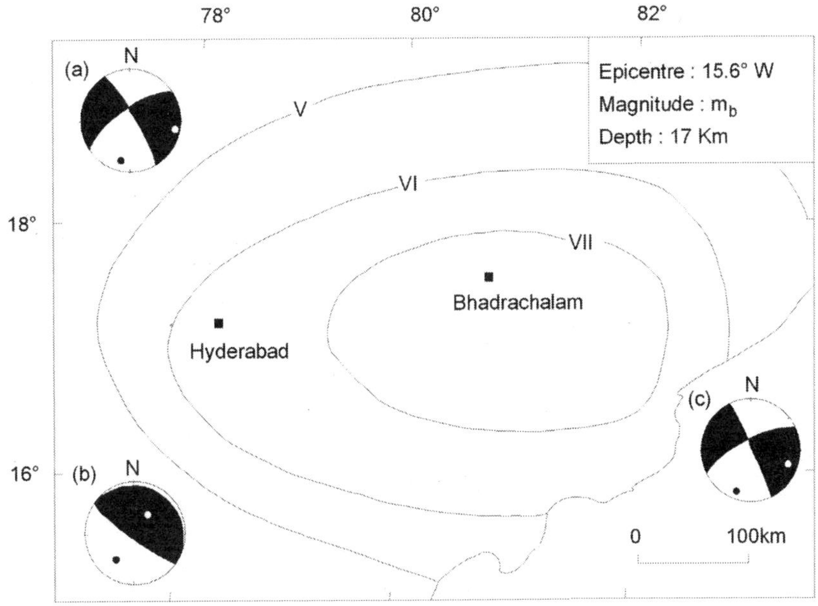

Fig. 7.35 Isoseismal map of the 1969 Bhadrachalam earthquake (GSI, 2000a) and fault plane solutions (a and b: Chandra, 1977; c: Chung, 1993).

7.4.11 Singhbhum Seismic Zone

The earthquake activity is northeast trending in this zone (Fig. 7.28), and it appears to merge with the intense activity of the Himalayan belt to the northeast. Among the significant past earthquakes, the January 23, 1866 Contai earthquake, intensity VI is described to have been accompanied by rumbling sound. Recently two significant earthquakes (M>5.0) are recorded in this zone; one in 1964 in Midnapore area and one in 1969 in Bankura area.

Midnapore Earthquake (M 5.5), 1964

The April 15, 1964 Midnapore earthquake M 5.5, was well felt at Kolkata (Calcutta) and other parts of West Bengal (Fig. 7.36). It was well recorded, and the epicentre was estimated at 21.7°N and 87.0°E with a focal depth at 36 km. A left lateral strike-slip solution was inferred for this event (Fig. 7.2).

Bankura Earthquake (M 5.7), 1969

The May 3, 1969 Bankura earthquake M 5.7, is another significant earthquake in this zone; epicentre was given at 23°N and 86.6°E (for location, Fig. 7.36). It was well felt in Kolkata (Calcutta) and in other parts of West Bengal.

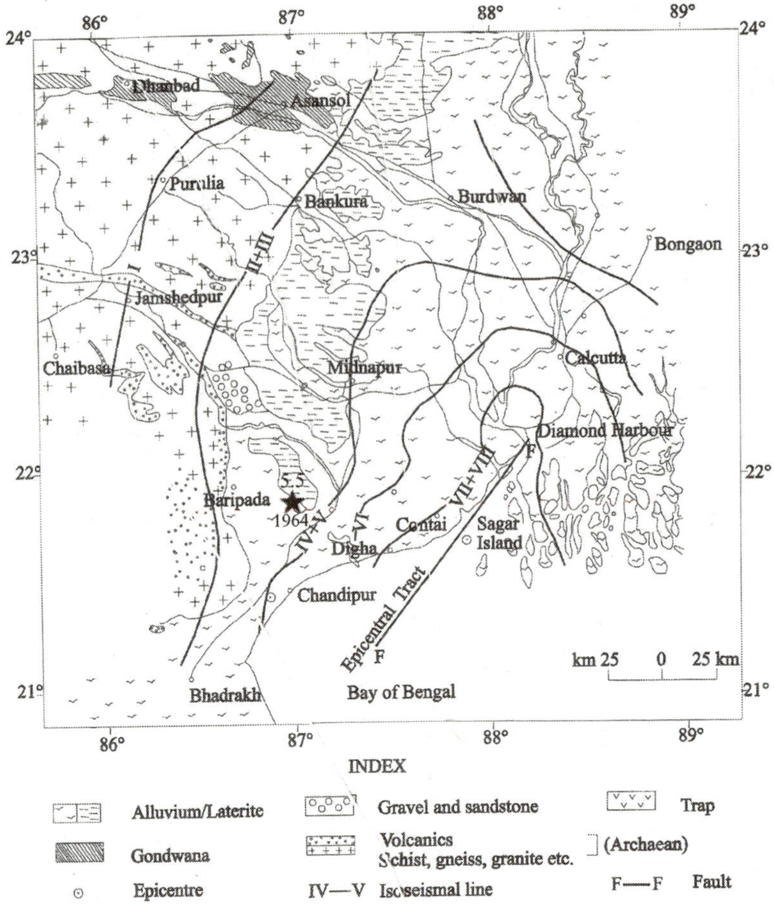

Fig. 7.36 Isoseismal map of the 1964 Midnapore earthquake (GSI, 2000a).

7.4.12 Killari Earthquake Zone

No such zone is classified in the identified seismic zones in peninsular India (Chandra, 1997) (Fig. 7.28). This zone is possibly the most conspicuous after the September 22, 1993 Killari earthquake M_W 6.1, M 6.3 in the eastern margin of the Deccan Plateau (Fig. 7.2). The zone represents a typical mid-cratonic SCR with subdued neotectonic expressions and low background seismicity. The 1993 Killari earthquake nucleated at a shallow depth (6 ± 1 km), and caused a loss about 10,000 human lives and huge property damages. Maximum intensity reached to IX (Fig. 7.37a). The fault plane solution shows a reverse faulting mechanism (Fig. 7.2). Many aftershocks were recorded, and details are given in Section 7.6.

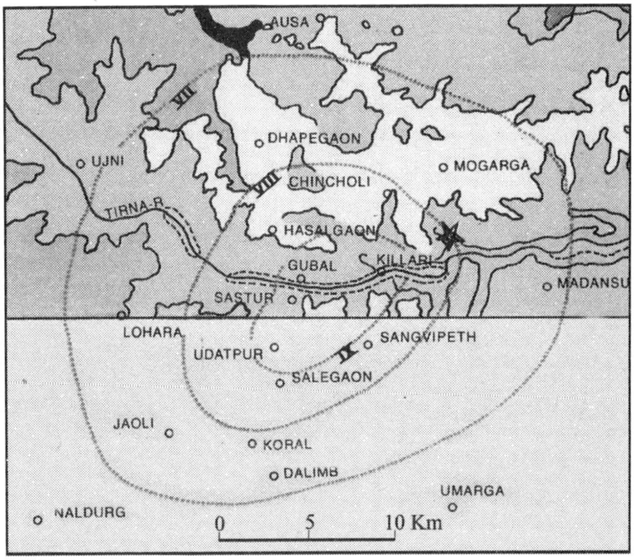

(a)

(b)

Fig. 7.37 (a) Sketch map of the isoseismals of the 1993 Killari earthquake (M_w 6.1), the main shock epicentre is shown by a black star. (b) Photograph shows the ground rupture and deformation in the epicentral area, Killari village (GSI, 1996).

About 1 km long rupture zone was identified in the Killari village area (Fig. 7.37). Trenching excavations across the rupture zone not only exposed fault plane, but also indicated repetition of movements. Preliminary observations, based on TL dating, suggest long recurrence intervals of the order of tens of thousands of years or more for the Killari type earthquake (Rajendran and Rajendran, 1997). Such long recurrence intervals are common for SCR earthquakes (e.g. Crone et al., 1992).

7.5 RECENT SEISMICITY: MICROEARTHQUAKE NETWORKS

Peninsular India although considered to be a stable landmass, various seismic activities are recorded during the last two decades. With the advent of microearthquake recording systems, seismicity in different parts of peninsular India is studied by many investigations. These investigations include monitoring Reservoir Induced Seismicity (RIS), swarm activity, foreshock and aftershock activities, active fault mapping etc. A brief discussion on these studies is made in this section.

7.5.1 Reservoir Induced Seismicity (Koyna Region)

Triggering of earthquakes by filling artificial reservoir water is known for over six decades (Gupta and Rastogi, 1976). Over 90 sites have been globally identified where earthquakes are reported to have triggered by such phenomena. In India, Koyna region has been identified to be the most significant and unique site for Reservoir Induced Seismicity (RIS), where the seismicity that began after the impoundment of a reservoir (Shivsagar lake behind the Koyna dam) in 1961 is persisting till to-date, since last more than 40 years (Gupta, 1992; Talwani, 1997). The first seismological observatory in Koyna region was established in 1963, but following the 1967 destructive earthquake a seismological network of seven stations was established during the years 1967-1972. Then another five-station network was established in 1990 in the Warna reservoir area, about 35 km south of the Koyna Dam. This is one of the regions in peninsular India which is well equipped with microearthquake networks for continuous monitoring of seismicity. In a recent review work, Gupta (2002) has given a detailed status of the Koyna-Warna reservoir seismicity, and he preferred to use the term Reservoir Trigger Seismicity (RTS) rather than RIS.

The December 10, 1967 Koyna earthquake, M 6.7, revised M_W 6.3, was believed to be the RIS (Gupta and Rastogi, 1976). The seismic activity is reported to have enhanced soon after the impoundment of the Koyna reservoir in 1962 and the Warna reservoir in 1992. Since then over 10 earthquakes $M \geq 5.0$, over 150 earthquakes $M \geq 4.0$ and over 100,000 events of $M \geq 0$ have occurred in this region (Gupta, 2002).

Talwani (1997) made a detailed study on the seismicity of the Koyna-Warna dam region using the analog data recorded from 1964 to 1995. The seismicity map (1964-1967) prior to the 1967 Koyna earthquake shows that the activity was confined in the Koyna dam area (Fig. 7.38a); the activity enhanced subsequently, and a NW-SE trend of activity was observed after the December 1967 earthquake during the period 1967-73 (Fig. 7.38b).

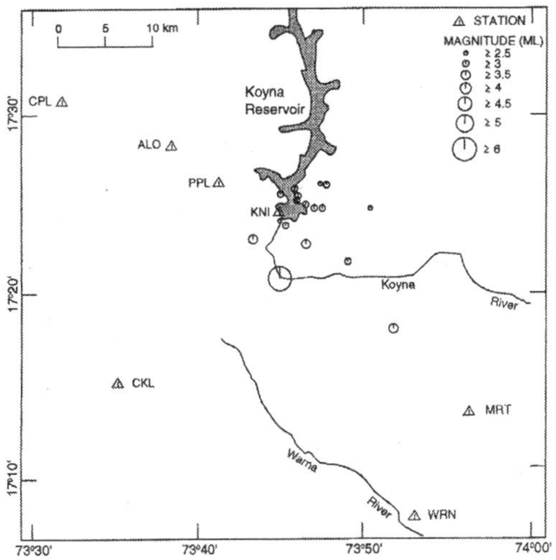

(a)

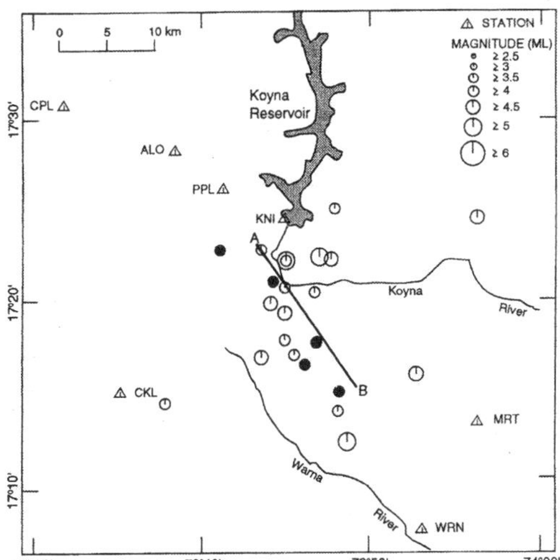

(b)

Fig. 7.38 (a) Relocated earthquakes (1964-1967), and epicentre of the December 10, 1967 Koyna earthquake; seismic stations are indicated by triangles, and (b) relocated earthquakes M>4.0 (December 10, 1967-1973) in the Koyna region; the aftershocks (solid circles) of the December 10, 1967 earthquake are aligned along the line AB. (Talwani, 1997).

Till 1992, the seismic activity was mostly confined to a 20 km long seismic zone extending south of Koyna dam (Fig. 7.38b). Two trends of seismicity, NW-SE and NE-SW, were, however, observed during 1993-1995 due to additional filling of the Warna reservoir located SSE of the Koyna dam at a distance of 35 km (Fig. 7.39a). The selected earthquakes (M>3) are shallow, within a depth range 5-15 km, mostly at a depth range 6-8 km. The seismicity is restricted by the Koyna River Fault Zone (KRFZ) to the west, that lies along the N-S portion of the Koyna river and extend to the south by atleast 40 km. The seismicity to the east is bounded by the NE-SW trending Patan fault, and the higher magnitude (M>5.0) earthquakes occurred within this zone (Fig. 7.39b). A similar observation of two seismicity trends was also made by Chadha et al. (1997), who relocated the lower magnitude (M<3.0) earthquakes in the region (Fig. 7.40a).

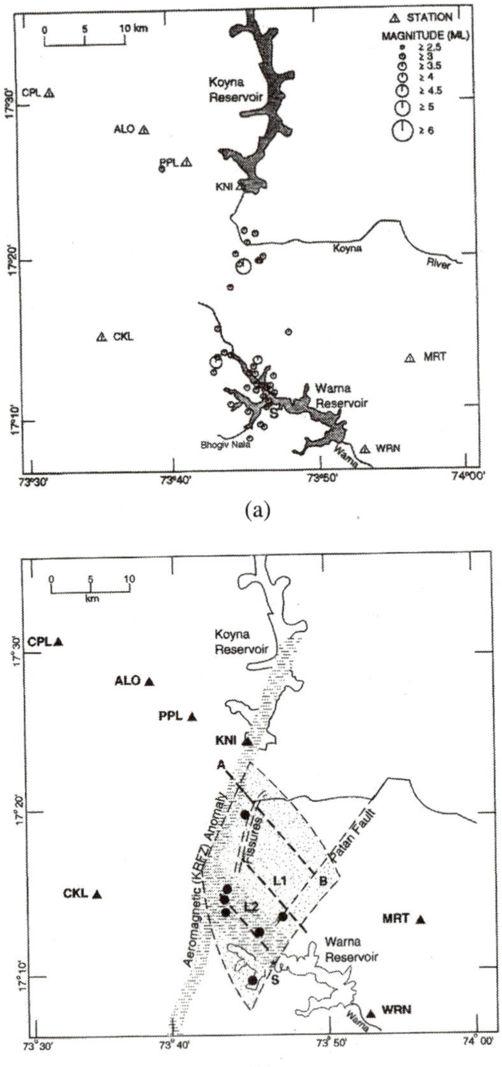

Fig. 7.39 (a) Relocated earthquakes (M>3.0) in Koyna-Warna region for 1993-95; seismic stations are indicated by triangles, and (b) interpreted structural elements of the Koyna-Warna region based on aeromagnetic, geological and seismicity data, the larger events M>5.0 are shown by solid circles (Talwani, 1997).

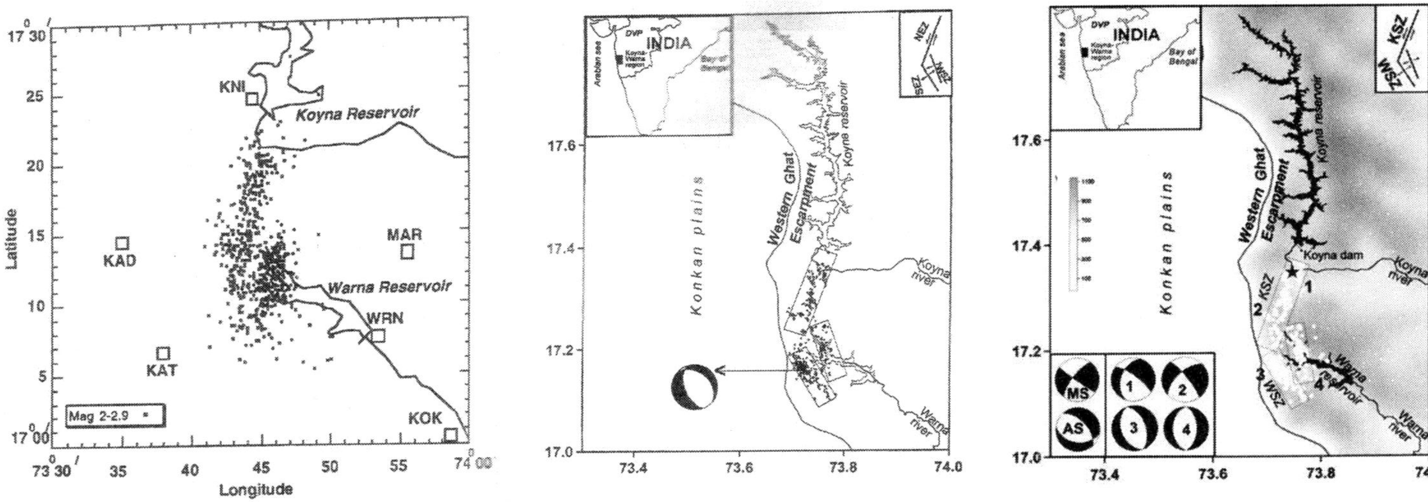

Fig. 7.40 (a) Koyna-Warna microseismicity, October, 1993-December, 1994, relocated by Chadha et al. (1997); seismic stations are shown by small rectangles, (b) microseismicity, April 1996-December 1997, located by a 10-station digital network (Rai et al., 1999b), and (c) the seismicity with fault plane solutions (Gahalaut et al., 2004).

An experiment was mounted deploying a 10-station digital seismic network during April, 1996 through December, 1997 (Rai et al., 1999b). A total of 20 sites over an area of 60 × 80 sq km were occupied by leap frogging with about 50% overlap of the seismic stations. They located 406 events within a zone of 11 × 25 sq km; depth distribution indicated that the base of the seismogenic zone is at ~10 km. They identified three seismic zones: north escarpment zone (NEZ), south escarpment zone (SEZ) and Warna seismic zone (WSZ) (Fig. 7.40 b).

Gahalaut et al. (2004), however, argued that the earthquakes in the Koyna-Warna region may be reservoir triggered, but the high seismicity is also influenced by the geometry of the fault zones and by their interactions through stress transfer. Two distinct fault zones were identified based on the distribution of epicentres and focal mechanisms of the earthquakes. The earthquakes occur by left lateral strike slip on the NNE-SSW trending faults in the Koyna Seismic Zone (KSZ), and by normal faulting on the NNW-SSE trending faults in the Warna Seismic Zone (WSZ) (Fig. 7.40c). They suggested that cumulative slip through occurrence of earthquakes on either of the two fault zones promote failure on the other. They further argued that the 1967 Koyna earthquake occurred by left-lateral strike-slip on the NNE-SSW trending fault (Langston, 1976), and occurrence of the largest aftershock (M 5.3) by normal faulting with slip on the NW-SE oriented plane (Langston and Franco-Sperra, 1985), that occurred 31 hours after the 1967 main Koyna earthquake supports this view (Fig. 7.40c).

7.5.2 Swarm Activity

Table 7.3 gives a list of 11 cases of earthquake swarm activity in peninsular India recorded since 1993. Out of these, three sequences are illustrated in Figs 7.41-7.43, that show burst of seismic activity for a short period, the activity then remains quiet for a longer time. The maximum magnitude of an earthquake in the sequence varied between 3.0 and 3.8 with no particular event as a main shock. The 1994 swarm activity at Medhi (Thane) near Bombay shows three burst of activities; in each burst the maximum magnitude of earthquake was of the order of M 3.0-3.7 (Fig. 7.41), and peak activity level reached about 80-100 events in a day. The swarm activity in Pandhana area during 1998-1999 is one of the longest sequences in central Indian tectonic zone (Fig. 7.42). The peak activity was recorded in October, 1998, with a maximum magnitude M 3.2. The 2001 Haripur swarm activity shows maximum activity in November with a maximum magnitude M 3.2 (Fig. 7.43).

In all the 11 cases listed in Table 7.3, it is observed that the starting month of commencing swarm activity was in the monsoon and post monsoon period between July and December. All the swarm activities were mostly recorded

Table 7.3: Examples of Swarm Activity in peninsular India (Bhattacharya and Dattatrayam, 2003)

Starting date	*Place/area Lat (°N), Lon (°E)*	*Opening period of Local observatory*	*Continued till*	*Total events recorded*	*Max. mag. and data*
1993 Dec. 1st week	Taklikalan, Bagmer (Khandwa Dt.) 21.7, 76.4	1993 Dec., 10-24	Dec. 24 (20 days)	118	2.6
1994 Jul. 27	-do-	1994 Aug. 7-1995 Mar. 31	Oct. 12 (2 mons. 15 days)	75	3.1 on Sep. 16
1994 Jan.	Medhi, (Jawahar Taluka (Thane Dt.) 19.8, 73.1	Dhamni obsy (MERI) existed.	Feb. end (2 months)	487	3.8 on Jan 9 (8 events of mag ≥ 3)
1994 Jul.	-do-	Dhamni obsy (MERI) existed, temp. obsy by IMD & NGRI	Oct. end (3 mons. 15 days)	1805	3.5 on Aug. 19 (12 events of mag ≥ 3)
1994 Aug.	Umarthana (Ratlam Dt.) 23.2, 74.9	1994 Aug. 10 - Oct. 24	Oct. 14 (2 mons. 15 days)	202	2.0 on Aug. 25
1995 Aug.	-do-	1995 Oct. 14-24	Oct. 24 (2 mons. 15 days)	36	2.7 on Oct. 14
1997 Dec. 9	Amarwara (Chhindwara Dt.) 22.3, 79.2	1997 Dec. 19-30	Dec. 30 (21 days)	24	3.2 on Dec. 21 (3 events of mag ≥ 3)
1998 Sept.	Sarangpur (Rajgarh Dt.) 23.6, 76.5	1998 Sep. 16-29	Sep. 29 (20 days)	121	1.2 on Sep. 26
1998 Sept. 11	Pandhana (Khandwa Dt.) 21.7, 76.2	1998 Sep. 17-1999 Feb. 12	1999 Jan. 27 (4 mons. 16 days) 101 events on Oct. 11	1601	3.2 on Oct. 20 (4 events of mag ≥ 3 with event Sep. 16)
1999 Oct. 01	-do-	1999 Oct. 25-Dec. 30	1999 Dec. 25 (2 mons. 25 days)	86	1.9 on Oct. 25
2001 Oct. 23	Haripur (Junagadh Dt.) 21.2, 70.5		2001 Dec. 28 (2 mons. 2 days) 145 events on Nov.10.	1689	3.2 on Nov. 11 (9 events of mag ≥ 3)

at shallower depth (0~3 km) with a maximum depth ~7 km for a few events. The activity is not only confined to a shallower depth but also to a smaller area. Shallow crustal heterogeneity and increase in pore-pressure by fluid flow normally caused the swarm activity. A detailed investigation of the Pandhana swarm activity is discussed below.

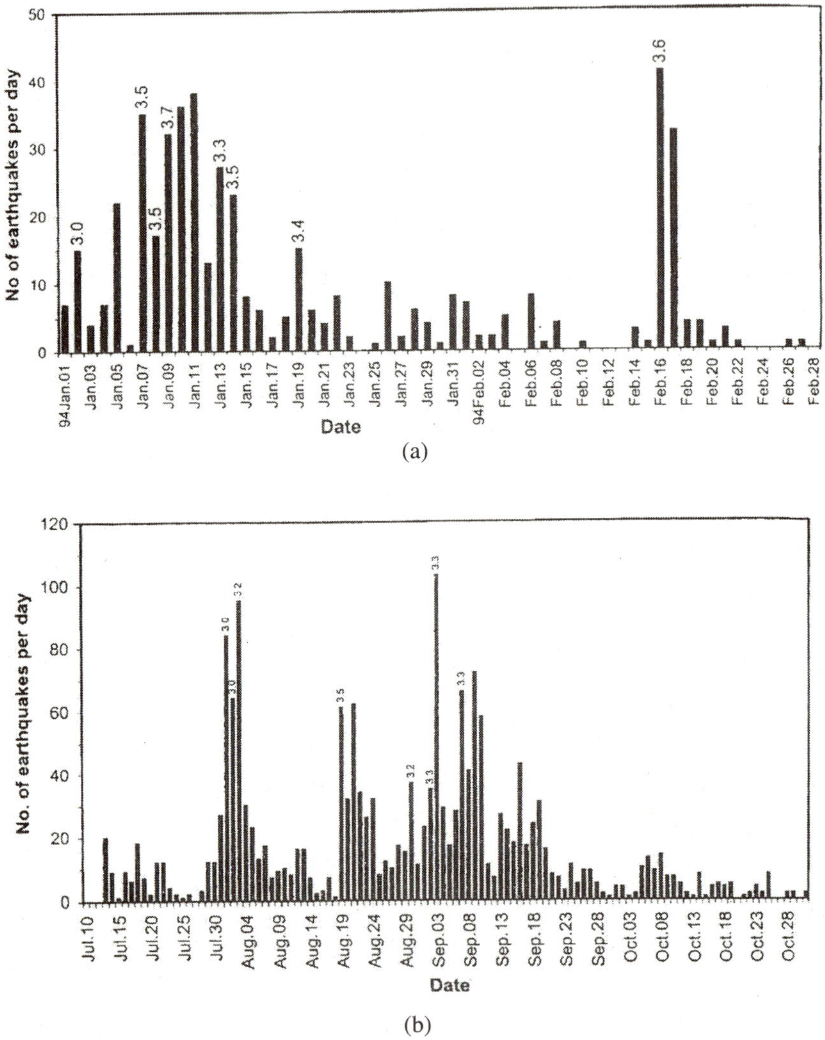

Fig. 7.41 Swarm at Medhi (Thane), (a) during January-February, 1994, and (b) during July-October, 1994 (Bhattacharya and Dattatrayam, 2003).

There is no mapped fault along the surface projection of the inferred seismogenic fault (Negishi et al., 2002; Kayal et al., 2002a). The aftershocks are mostly confined to deeper depths (12-37 km). A similar observation of the 1811-12 New Madrid large earthquake was reported (Hough et al., 2002); these findings suggest that such large intraplate earthquake can occur by hidden fault(s) without producing surface rupture. The main shock and the aftershocks occurred in a high velocity block filled with fluid (?), this is similar to that observed for other large earthquakes in the world (Mendoza and Hartzell, 1988; Zhao et al., 2002). The precise locations and fault-plane solutions provide a new insight into the Bhuj earthquake source processes. The rupture propagation and different fault-plane solutions with depth, space and time are well reflected by the aftershocks.

Lateral heterogeneity as well as complex velocity structure, a high velocity and low velocity contact zone at a shallow depth (7 km ± 1 km), (Fig. 7.49), was reported to be the source area for the 1993 Killari earthquake (m_b 6.3), a damaging intraplate earthquake in central India (Kayal and Mukhopadhyay, 2002). Hauksson and Haase (1994) reported four earthquakes (M>5.9) in the Los Angles basin, California, at the boundary between low and high velocity zones; they interpreted that the high velocity zone forms the upper block of a thrust fault. A similar observation is reported for the 2001 Bhuj earthquake source area (Kayal et al., 2002b; Mandal et al., 2004), and it is supported by gravity and magnetic observations (Chandrasekhar and Mishra, 2002; Chandrasekhar et al., 2004 and Mishra et al., 2005).

Kayal et al. (2002b) inferred that the rocks of lower rigidity or the fluid-filled rock matrix might have contributed to the initiation of the Bhuj main shock. Zhao et al. (2002) reported the role of fluid/magma filled rocks in nucleation of earthquakes in Japan. Mishra and Zhao (2003) reported high crack density, high porosity and high saturation in the Bhuj earthquake source area. Ray (2004), on the other hand, suggested that activation of a fault that causes a large earthquake generates enough flush heat to melt the fragmented rocks at the frictional interfaces. The block structures, velocity heterogeneity and melt rock (?)/fluid filled rock (?) in the source area are, however, imaged after the main shock. The fluid filled (?) or melt rock (?) in source area may be a pre-earthquake or a post-earthquake phenomena. This phenomena cannot be resolved unless both the pre-earthquake (main shock) and post earthquake tomography studies are made.

The Kutch paleorift basin comprises a series of uplifts, master faults and up-thrusts (Fig. 7.53). Biswas (1987) postulated that the uplifts are the result of the differential movements of discrete basement blocks due to compression along these faults. Ravishanker (1995) suggested that differential thermal and crustal structures provide the motive force for relative movements between various crustal blocks under the NNE-SSW compressive stress due to northward movement of the Indian plate. Pre-earthquake and post-earthquake gravity and magnetic study confirmed a block uplift in the source area (Chandrasekhar and Mishra, 2002; Mishra et al., 2005). A coseismic displacement of 16±8 mm at N35°E during the Bhuj earthquake is reported by Jade et al. (2002) from GPS (1997) - GPS (2001) measurement at Jamnagar. The Jamnagar area is about 150 km south of the main shock epicentre, and lies on the hanging wall of the reverse fault that caused the earthquake. This indicates that the post seismic deformation controls this shortening. They further reported shortening of the baseline lengths of five GPS points within the KRB irrespective of their orientation relative to the NNE-SSW compressional direction.

7.7 SRI LANKA: TECTONIC CONFIGURATION

Rifting between India and Sri Lanka

Since the breakup of the Indian subcontinent from Gondwanaland in early Cretaceous, its kinship with Madagascar, Sri Lanka, Antarctica and Australia has been a fascinating geo-scientific problem. It was suggested that unlike the present geographical positions, southeast India and northwest Sri Lanka were once a single landmass (Katz, 1974, 1978a, b). He suggested two proto-boundary faults with a separation of about 200 km between the two landmasses, which earlier closed up the Gulf of Mannar and Palk Strait (Fig. 7.59).

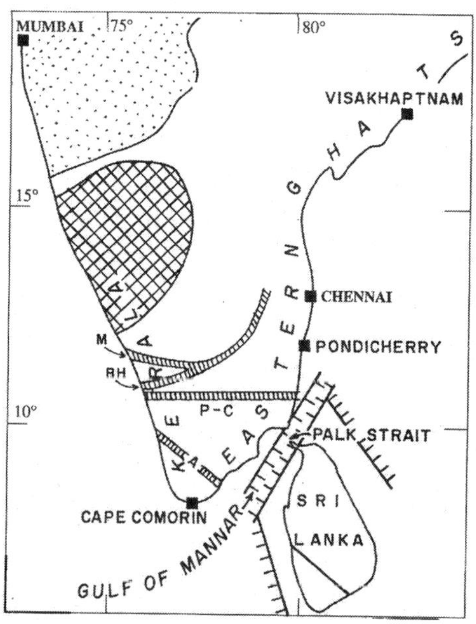

Fig. 7.59 Present position of Sri Lanka with respect to India. M: Moyar, BH: Bhavani, P-C: Palaghat-Cauvery and A: Achankovil shear zones respectively (Agarwal and Pandey, 1999).

Yoshida et al. (1992), however, pointed out the juxtaposition of Sri Lanka with Lutzow-Holm Bay of Antarctica (Fig. 7.60), that required 80 km northward movement and 30° clockwise rotation of Sri Lanka from its present position. This assembly shows a good correlation of geological units among peninsular India, Sri Lanka and east Antarctica. It was hypothesized that the Palk Strait is a triple junction that joined the east coast of India at Cape Comorin in the west and Pondicherry in the east.

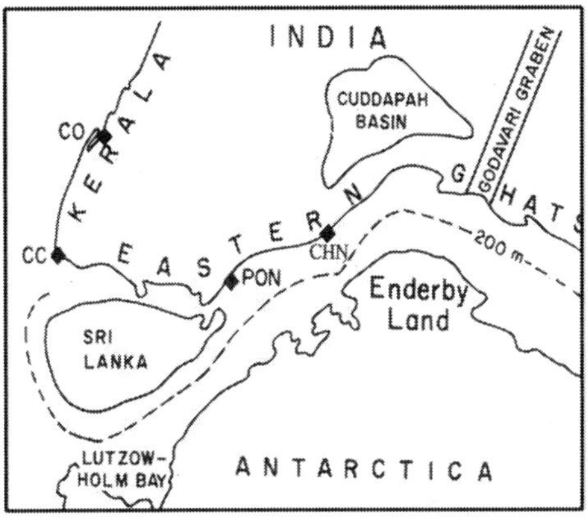

Fig. 7.60 Pre-break up position of Sri Lanka with respect to Antarctica and India (Yoshida et al., 1992). CO: Cochin, CC: Cape Comorin, PON: Pondicherry and CHN: Chennai (Madras).

Volcanism

Continental break up are normally associated with surface magmatism (Courtillot et al., 1999); for example Rajmahal traps reflect the break up of India from Antarctica at ~115 Ma. Cretaceous flood basalts of Madagascar are related to the break up of Madagascar from Dharwar craton, south India at ~88 Ma (Storey et al., 1995), Deccan traps to the break up of Seychelles from west coast of India at ~65 Ma. No such volcanism is, however, reported with the break up (?) of Sri Lanka from India. The 200 m isobath around the east coast of India and Sri Lanka, on the other hand, indicates non-oceanic crust between the two.

Gravity Anomaly

Based on Bouguer gravity anomaly (Fig. 7.61), Agarwal and Pandey (1999) suggested that the gentle nature of anomalies with a few closures near the east coast of India does not support any rifting or a fault below the east coast area. The continuation and one to one correspondence of gravity contours between Sri Lanka and India, on the other hand, suggest an identical nature of crust or lithosphere below the two areas.

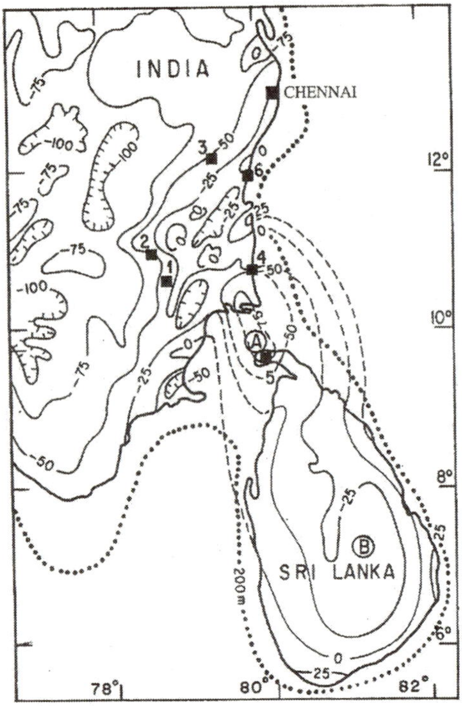

Fig. 7.61 Bouguer anomaly (mGal) map of southeast Indian shield and Sri Lanka (Agarwal and Pandey, 1999). 1. Nartamali, 2. Tiruchirapalli, 3. Gingee, 4. Nagapattinam, 5. Jaffna peninsula, 6. Pondicherry. A: gravity anomaly over Palk Srait, B: gravity anomaly over eastern Vijayan series, Sri Lanka.

The gravity anomaly -75 mGal marked as A over the Palk Srait, between Nagapattinam in the east of India and Jaffna peninsula of Sri Lanka strikes almost right angle to the east coast of India. Agarwal and Pandey (1999) suggested that this could be the result of asthenosheric upwelling during the break up between Antarctica and India at ~130 Ma and Marion hot spot activity at ~90Ma. Another anomaly of -25 mGal, marked as B (Fig. 7.61), over eastern Vijayan group of rocks may be a local anomaly, and does not seem to have any apparent relationship with the break up or rifting.

Magnetic Anomaly

Reddi et al. (1988) prepared a total intensity map of peninsular India region, south of 12° latitude (Fig. 7.62). They adopted 2D low pass filtering that resulted in a predominantly longer wavelength essentially reflecting the deeper structures. The gentle nature of the magnetic contours does not suggest any rift structure at the east coast.

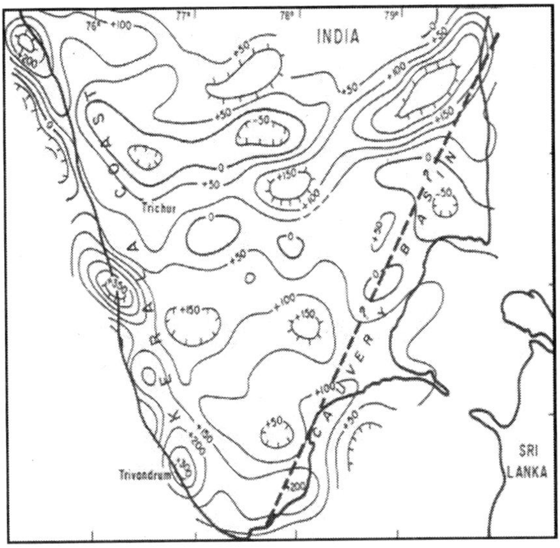

Fig. 7.62 Long wave length total intensity magnetic map of south India (Reddi et al., 1988); thick dashed line indicates protoboundary fault proposed by Katz (1978a).

In the west coast, on the other hand, the trends are clearly suggestive of faulting parallel to the Kerala coast. It may be worth mentioning that some of the NW-SE mega-lineaments in south India seem to be extending to Sri Lanka (Fig. 7.63).

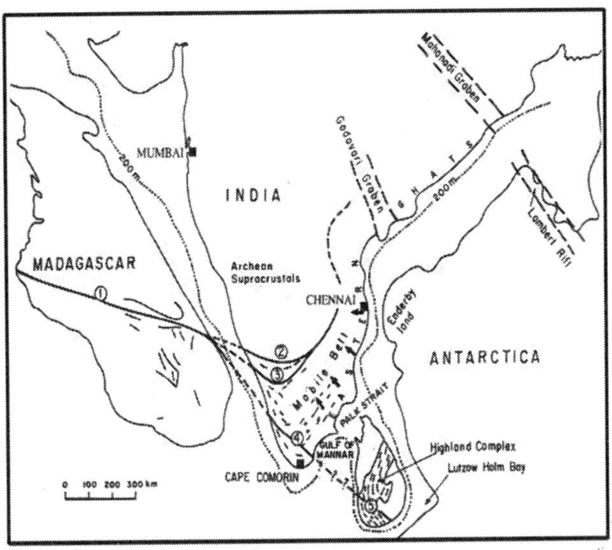

Fig. 7.63 Correlations between Madagascar, India, Sri Lanka and Antarctica (Agarwal et al. 1992). 1. Bongolava-Ranotsara lineament, 2. Moyar shear zone, 3. Bhavani shear zone, 4. Achankovil shear zone, 5. major fault/lineament in Sri Lanka (Katz, 1978b, Vitanage, 1986).

Seismicity

Seismicity of south India (Rao, 1992) and microearthquake epicentres in Sri Lanka (Fernando and Kulasinghe, 1986) are shown in Fig. 7.64. The proposed protoboundary faults over the two landmasses are also shown. No seismicity is observed along the proposed protoboundary faults. A higher degree of seismicity is, observed at the latitude 12-14°N in south India, which may be due to structural heterogeneities in the area. In Sri Lanka, there is not much seismic activity; microseismicity is observed in the geologically complex southern part, that is bounded by two lineaments, and practically no seismicity is observed in the north. Only one permanent BB station (part of the GSN) is now in operation in the southern part of Sri Lanka since last one decade. The ISC catalog recorded some five earthquakes M 4.5-5.0 in the last 100 years, one in the main land of Sri Lanka (Fig. 7.64) and rest in the surrounding ocean floor of Sri Lanka, which could be attributed to intraplate earthquakes in this region.

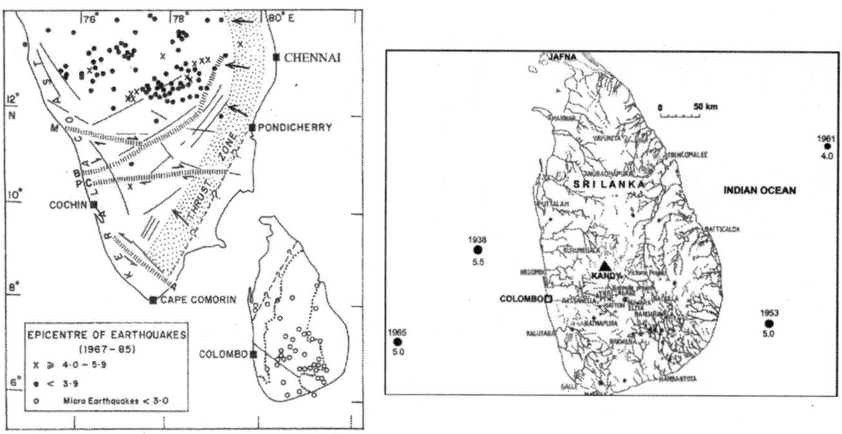

Fig. 7.64 (a) Epicentral distribution of earthquakes in southern India (Rao, 1992) and in Sri Lanka (Fermando and Kulasinghe, 1986). (b) Geomorphological map of Sri Lanka with epicentres of earthquakes (M > 4.0) in and around Sri Lanka (Agarwal and Pandy, 1999).

Tectonic Interpretaion

The above evidences suggest that Sri Lanka remained a part of super peninsular India, occupying the similar position as it was having in the erstwhile Gondwanaland about 180 Ma ago (Fig. 7.60). The two fragments accompanied each other throughout their geodynamic mobility after they broke away from Antarctica at ~130 Ma ago. The paleo-assembly seems reasonable as evidenced by the present geological, tectonic and geophysical information (Fig. 7.63). The magsat and gravity data suggest that Madagascar was a part of Dharwar craton of south India and the Bhavani lineament matches well with the Bongolava-Ranotsara lineament in Madagascar (Fig. 7.63). Similarly, there is a possibility that the Lambert rift (Antarctica) joins the Mahanadi graben in India (Fig. 7.63). Burke and Dewey (1973b) anticipated the presence of triple junctions at Gulf of Mannar and Cambay, and it matches well with the concept of Marion and Reunion plume outburst at about 89 Ma and 65 Ma respectively which resulted in the separation of Madagascar and Seychelles from greater India.

It appears that before the break up of the Gondwanaland. the island of Sri Lanka rested in the Lutzow-Holm Bay, and its paleo-position with respect to India may have been same as it is now, although a small scale rotational movement may not be ruled out as suggested by Yoshida et al. (1992). Sri Lanka and India travelled together to its present position, the available geological and geophysical data do not support rifting between the two landmasses or existence of protoboundary faults. Seismically the island of Sri Lanka typically falls in the category of SCR. Although there is no historical record of large earthquake in Sri Lanka, which is limited only for 100-150 years, occurrence of strong intraplate earthquake M ~6.0 in Sri Lanka cannot be ruled out. Recurrence period of such SCR earthquake is normally of the order of 1000 years, and we have no historical data to be sure that such event never happened in Sri Lanka unless verified by some paleoseismological studies.

7.8 CONCLUSION AND RECOMMENDATION

The Indian peninsular shield is no longer considered to be a 'stable land' or seismically inactive as was shown in the seismic zonation map earlier (Fig. 2.19). The devastating earthquakes in the recent past, like the 1967 Koyna earthquake (M 6.7), 1993 Killari earthquake (m_b 6.3), 1997 Jabalpur earthquake (M 6.0) and the most devastating 2001 Bhuj earthquake (M_w 7.7) have radically changed the seismic zonation map of India (Fig. 2.20).

Significantly enhanced activity of moderate magnitude earthquakes (M $\simeq$ 6.0) in recent years compared to that in the past century (Gaur, 2003) called for modernisation of the national network (IMD) and for enough fund and instruments for digital microearthquake networks, stand alone seismic stations/temporary networks around the country. In this chapter, it has been attempted to highlight the results of temporary stations/network data to shed light in understanding of the intraplate seismicity in peninsular India.

Among the four damaging earthquakes mentioned above, the 1967 Koyna and the 1993 Killari earthquakes are the typical shield earthquakes, originated at shallower depth (<10 km) by reactivation of thrust/reverse fault(s). Seismic tomography study revealed crustal heterogeneities, and it is observed that the existing faults had been the source areas for these earthquakes.

The 1997 Jabalpur and the 2001 Bhuj earthquakes, on the other hand, are found to be generated at deeper depths (25-35 km), at the base of the paleo-rift zones, NRB and KRB respectively, by reactivation of the existing surface faults and/or hidden faults. The normal faults of these rifts developed in the geological past are now reactivating as reverse faults due to accumulation of compressional stress at the fault end by the plate movements.

In addition to the detailed aftershock study and review of a few strong earthquakes M~6.0 in peninsular India, several studies on RTS, active faults, swarm activity are made by microearthquake networks, that have shed more light on the earthquake processes in different tectonic blocks of the shield area.

The results of these investigations revealed that the SCR seismicity occur in the vicinity of stress concentrators in the pre-existing hidden fault zones and failed rift zones. The stress concentrators include intersecting faults, heterogeneity in velocity structures at the fault end, rift pillows etc. The SCR seismicity have longer return periods compared to their plate boundary counterparts. Talwani and Gangopadhyay (2003) studied about 40 SCR earthquakes around the world and suggested that the earthquakes occur in failed rifts of all ages, whereas those not associated with failed rifts occur only in the Precambrian crust. The failed rift earthquakes are deeper (~20-30 km) and have shorter return periods (~500 years), the Precambrian crust events, on the other hand, are shallower (~10 km) and have longer return periods (~1000 years).

Our knowledge in seismotectonics is, however, limited to a few earthquakes in peninsular India; much remains to be done. Our present national network (IMD) is capable to locate earthquakes M≥4.0. The capability on the national network needs to be increased to locate earthquakes down to M 3.0. This would require more close-spaced (<100 km) seismic stations in the country compared to the present 150-200 km spacing of the stations in the national network. In the earthquake prone/high risk zones, telemetry systems need to be implemented and in some areas the existing networks need to be upgraded. Permanent digital telemetry and stand alone digital seismic network data need to be analysed by R&D (Research and Development) effort more rigorously not only for tectonic study but also for precursor study.

The seismic tomography study is only limited to the Killari and Bhuj earthquake source areas. We did very little to understand the deep crustal structure of the continent except a few studies on receiver function analysis. We need to have high precision large quantity digital data set of the whole country to bring out detailed seismic images at least down to the mantle depth for identification of the earthquake source areas for hazard mitigation. This is an important task for the future seismologists. There are now about 50 permanent BB stations in peninsular India that are run by various organizations for about five to six years, these data are although used to some extent for receiver function analysis, no effort is made yet for detailed seismic tomography study to identify the earthquake source areas beneath the shield area. Seismic tomography may shed light on the hidden seismogenic structures, fault(s), velocity heterogeneities, stress concentrators etc. beneath the crust. This should be a challenge for the future seismologists.

Several international projects are now taken up for seismological studies in the country. Our future research should focus not only on the seismotectonics of the earthquakes but also on the crustal deformation studies by the GSP measurements, microzonation, seismic hazard studies etc. Real time monitoring of earthquakes is very much essential; our national network needs to be upgraded for this purpose immediately. Along with high precision seismic data/networks, earthquake precursor studies should be taken up as a challenging task in future. Multi-parameter observatory should be established in seismically active zones to monitor seismological, geophysical, geochemical and geodetic precursors. Finally, it is an indisputable fact that although we develop modernisation or scientific knowledge to understand earthquake genesis or its source areas, it is the adequate engineering knowledge and capabilities to construct or design human habitats that would provide less human loss. Earthquakes do not kill people, it is the poorly constructed houses that kill people. We have had enough experience of this ignorance in 1993 Killari earthquake or in 1997 Jabalpur and 2001 Bhuj earthquakes. Even if the scientists are able to answer when and where the next earthquake might strike, it may save human lives, but not the man-made properties, houses and buildings, which are not properly constructed. Knowledge of seismology and seismotectonics may shed light on our understanding of earthquakes, but cannot prevent the earthquakes to occur.

References

Abercrombie, R.E., Antolik, M. and Ekstrom, G., 2003. The June 2000 Mw 7.9 earthquake south of Sumatra: Deformation in the India-Australia plate. *J. Geophys. Res.*, **108(B),** 2018, doi: 10.1029/2001JB 000674.

Acharyya, S.K., 1986. Tectono stratigraphic history of Naga hill ophiolites. *Geol. Surv. India Mem.*, **119,** 94-103.

Acharyya, S.K., Ghosh, S.C. and Ghosh, R.N., 1983. Geological framework of the eastern Himalaya in parts of Kameng, Subansiri, Siang districts, Arunachal Pradesh. *Geol. Surv. India Misc. Pub.*, **43,** 145-152.

Acharyya, S.K., Mitra, N.D. and Nandy, D.R., 1986. Regional geology and tectonic setting of northeast India and adjoining region. *Geol. Surv. India Mem.*, **119,** 61-72.

Acharyya, S.K., Kayal, J.R., Roy, A. and Chaturvedi, R.K., 1998. Jabalpur earthquake of May 22, 1997: Constraint from aftershock study. *J. Geol. Soc. India*, **51,** 295-304.

Adams, R.D., 1979. T-phase recordings at Rarotonga from underground nuclear explosion. *Geophys. J .R. Astro. Soc.*, **58,** 361-369.

Agarwal, B.N.P., Das, L.K., Chakraborty, K. and Sivaji, CH., 1995. Analysis of the Bouguer anomaly over Central India: A regional perspective. *Geol. Soc. India Mem.*, **31,** 469-493.

Agarwal, P.K. and Pandey, O.P., 1999. Was there an intercontinental rift between India and Sri Lanka? *J. Geol. Soc. India*, **54,** 237-249.

Agarwal, P.K., Pandey, O.P. and Negi, J.G., 1992. Madagascar: A continental fragment of the paleosuper Dharwar craton of India. *Geology*, **20,** 543-546.

Agarwal, R.K., 1977. Structure and tectonics of Indo Gangetic Plains – Geophysical case histories of India. *J. Asoc. Expl. Geophys.*, **1,** 29-46.

Airy, G.B, 1855. On the computations of the effect of the attraction of the mountain Manes as disturbing the apparent astronomical latitude of stations in geodetic surveys. *Phil. Trans. Roy. Soc*. London, **14,** 101.

Aki, K., 1965. Maximum-likelihood estimate of b in the formula log N = a – bM and its confidence limits. *Bull. Earthquake Res. Inst.*, Tokyo Univ., **43,** 237-239.

Aki, K., 1966. Earthquake generating stress in Japan for the years 1961 to 1963 obtained by smoothing the first motion radiation patterns. *Bull. Earthquake Res. Inst.*, Tokyo Univ., **44,** 447-471.

Aki, K., 1988. Local site effects on strong ground motion. *Proc. Earthquake Engg. Soil Dyn.*, 103-155.

Aki, K., and Lee, W.H.K., 1976. Determination of three dimensional velocity anomalies under a seismic array using first P arrival times from local earthquakes: A homogeneous initial model. *J. Geophys. Res.*, **81,** 4381-4399.

Aki, K. and Richards, P.G., 1980. *Methods of Quantitative Seismology*, Freeman, California.

Aki, K., Christoffersson, A. and Husebye, E.S., 1977. Determination of three dimensional seismic structure of the lithosphere. *J. Geophys. Res.*, **82,** 277-296.

Allegre, C.J. et al., 1984. Structure and evolution of the Himalaya-Tibet Organic Belt. *Nature*, **307,** 17-22.

Ambraseys, N.N., 2000. Reappraisal of north Indian earthquakes at the turn of the 20th century. *Curr. Sci.*, **79,** 101-114.

Ambraseys, N.N. and Bilham, Roger, 2003. Reevaluated intensities for the Great Assam earthquake of 12th June 1897, Shillong, India. *Bull. Seism. Soc. Am.*, **93(2),** 655-673.

Ambraseys, N.N. and Douglas, J., 2004. Magnitude calibration of north Indian earthquakes. *Geophys. J. Int.*, **159,** 165-206.

Ammon, C.J., 1991. The isolation of receiver effects from teleseismic P waveforms. *Bull. Seism. Soc. Am.*, **81,** 2504-2510.

Ammon, C.J., Ji, C., Thio, H., Robinson, D., Ni, S., Hjorteifsdottir., Kanamori, H., Lay, T., Das, S., Helmberger, D., Ichinose, G., Polet, J. and Wald, D., 2005. Rupture process of the 2004 Sumatra-Andaman earthquake. *Science*, **308,** 1133-1139.

Anderson, E.M., 1951. *The dynamics of faulting and dyke formation with applications to Britain.* 2nd ed., Oliver and Boyd, London.

Anderson, J.A. and Wood, H.O. 1925. Description and theory of the torsion seismometer. *Bull. Seism. Soc. Am.*, **15,** 1-72.

Angulo-Brown, F., Ramirez-Guzman, A.H., Yepez, E., Rudiof-Navarroa, A. and Pavia-Miller, C.G., 1998. Fractal geometry and seismicity in the Mexican subduction zone. *Geofisica International*, **37,** 29-33.

Antolik, M. and Dreger, D.S., 2003. Rupture process of the 26 January 2001 Mw 7.6 Bhuj, India earthquake from teleseismic broadband data. *Bull. Seism. Soc. Am.*, **93,** 1235-1248.

Appa Rao, M., Sastri, C.B.K. and Reddy, R.A., 1996. Gravity, magnetic and resistivity investigations around Killari. *Geol. Surv. India Sp. Pub.*, **37,** 193-214.

Argand, E., 1924. La Tectonic de I'Asie. *Int. Geol. Cong. Rep.*, **13(1),** 170-732.

Armijo, R., Tapponnier, P., and Han, T., 1989. Late Cenozoic right-lateral strike-slip faulting in southern Tibet. *J. Geophys. Res.*, **94,** 2787-2838.

Armijo, R., Tapponnier, P., Mercirr, J.L. and Han, T., 1986. Quaternary extension in southern Tibet: Field observations and tectonic implications. *J. Geophys. Res.*, **91,** 13803-13872.

Armstrong, B.H., 1969. Acoustic emission prior to rock bursts and earthquakes. *Bull. Seism. Soc. Am.*, **59,** 1259-1279.

Arora, B.R. and Singh, B.P., 1992. Geomagnetic and geoelectric investigations for seismicity and seismotectonics of the Himalayan region. *In:* Himalayan Seismicity, G.D Gupta (ed.), *Geol. Soc. India Mem.*, **23,** 1-21.

Arya, A.S., 2000. Recent development towards earthquake risk development. *Curr. Sci.*, **79,** 1270-1277.

Asada, T., 1957. Observations of nearby microearthquakes with ultrasensitive seismometers. *J. Phys. Earth*, **5,** 83-113.

Assumpcao, M. and Suarez, G., 1988. Source mechanisms of moderate size earthquakes and stress orientation in mid-plate South America. *Geophys. J. Int.*, **92,** 253-267.

Atchuta Rao, D., Sanker Narayan, P.V. and Hari Narain, 1970. A study of the aeromagnetic profiles across the Cuddapah basin, *Geophys. Res. Bull.*, **8,** 11-25.

Avouac, J.P. and Tapponier, P., 1993. Kinemetic model of active deformation in central Asia. *Geophys. Res. Lett.*, **20,** 895-898.

Avouac, J.P., Tapponier, P., Bai, M., You, H. and Wang, G., 1993. Active thrusting and folding along the northern Tien Shan and Cenozoic rotation of the Tarim relative to Dzingaria and Kazakhstan. *J. Geophys. Res.*, **98,** 6755-6804.

Avouac, J.P., Ayoub, F., Leprince, S., Konca, O. and Helmberger, D.V., 2006. The 2005 Mw 7.6 Kashmir earthquake: Sub-pixel correlation of ASTER images and seismic waveform analysis. *Earth Planet Sci. Lett.*, **249,** 514-528.

Bacon, C.F., 1975. Acoustic emission along San Andreas fault in southern central California. *Calif. Geol.*, **28,** 147-154.

Baksi, S.K., 1965. Stratiography of Barail series in southern part of Shillong Plateau, Assam, India. *Am. Assoc. Pet. Geol. Bull.*, **49,** 2282-2294.

Bakun, W.H. and Lindh, A.G., 1977. Local magnitudes, seismic moments and coda durations for earthquakes near Oroville, California. *Bull. Seism. Soc. Am.*, **67,** 615-629.

Balakrishnan, S., Christopher, G. and Rama Rao, A.V., 1967. Regional magnetic and gravity studies over Cuddapah basin. Proc. UMP Symp., Hyderabad, GRB & NGRI Publ. No. 8, pp. 303-319.

Banerjee, B. and Shaw, R.K., 2001. Marine magnetic anomalies near the Barren Islands volcano, Andaman sea. *Curr. Sci.*, **81,** 816-818.

Banerjee, P. and Bürgmann, R., 2002. Convergence across the northwest Himalaya from GPS measurements, *Geophys. Res. Lett.*, **29(13),** 30.1-30.4.

Banerjee, P., Pollitz, F.F. and Burgmann, R., 2005. The size and duration of the Sumatra-Andaman earthquake from far-field static offsets. *Science*, **308,** 1769-1772.

Banghar, A.R., 1990. Mechanism solutions of two recent Indian earthquakes. Symposium on Recent Advances in Seismology and their Applications, Abs. vol., Bangalore, India, July 16-19.

Banghar, A.R., 1991. Mechanism solution of Nepal-Bihar earthquake of August 20, 1988. *J. Geol. Soc. India*, **37,** 25-30.

Bapat, A., Kulkarni, R.C. and Guha, S.K., 1983. Catalogue of earthquakes in India and neighbourhood from historical record up to 1979. Indian Soc. Earthq. Tech., Roorkee, 211 p.

Baranowski, J., Armbruster, J., Seeber, L. and Molnar, P., 1984. Focal depths and fault plane solutions of earthquakes and active tectonics of the Himalaya. *J. Geophy. Res.*, **89,** 6918-6928.

Barazangi, M. and Ni, J., 1982. Velocities and propagation characteristics of Pn and Sn beneath the Himalayan arc and Tibetan Plateau: Possible evidence for understanding of the Indian continental lithosphere beneath Tibet. *Geology*, **10,** 179-185.

Båth, M., 1973. *Introduction to Seismology*, Birkhauser Verlag. Basel, 355 p.

Båth, M., 1979. *Introduction to Seismology*, Birkhauser Verlag. Basel, 428 p.

Båth, M. and Shahidi, M., 1974. T phase from Atlantic earthquakes. *Pure and Appl. Geophys.*, **94,** 74-114.

Baumbach, M., Grosser, H., Schmidt, H.G., Paulat, A., Rietbrock, A., Rao, C.V.R., Raju, P.S., Sarkar, D. and Mohan, I. 1994. Study of the foreshocks and aftershocks of the intraplate Latur earthquake of September 30, 1993, India. *Geol. Soc. India Mem.*, **35,** 33-63.

Behera, L., Sain, K. and Reddy, P.R., 2004. Evidence of underplating from seismic and gravity studies in the Mahanadi delta of eastern India and its tectonic significance. *J. Geoph. Res.*, **109,** B12311, doi: 10.1029/2003 JB 002764.

Beloussov, V.V., Belyaevsky, N.A., Borsov, A.A., Volvovsky, B.S., Volvovsky, I.S., Resvoy, D.P., Talvirsky, B.B., Khamrabaev, I.Kh., Kaila, K.L., Hari Narain, Marussi, A. and Finetti, J., 1980. Structure of the lithosphere along the deep seismic sounding profile. Tien-Shan Pamirs-Karakorum-Himalayas. *Tectonophysics*, **70,** 193-221.

Ben Menahem, A., Aboodi, E. and Schild, R., 1974. The source of the great Assam earthquake – An interplate wedge motion. *Phys. Earth Planet. Inter.*, **9,** 265-289.

Bender, F., 1983. Geology of Burma. Borntrager, Berlin, 293 p.

Bendick, R., Bilham, R., Fielding, E., Gaur, V.K., Hough, S.E., Keir, G., Kulkarni, M.N., Martin, S., Mueller, K. and Mukul, M., 2001. The 26 January "Republic Day" Earthquake, India. *Seism. Res. Lett.*, **72(3),** 328-335.

Bevis, M. and Isacks, B.L., 1984. Hypocentral trend surface analysis: Probing the geometry of Wadati-Benioff zones. *J. Geophys. Res.*, **89,** 6153-6170.

Bhatia, S.C., Kumar, R. and Gupta, H.K., 1999. A probabilistic seismic hazard map of India and adjoining regions (GSHAP). *Curr. Sci.*, **77(3),** 447-450.

Bhattacharya, Pankaj M. and Kayal, J.R., 2003. Mapping the b-value and its correlation with the fractal dimension in the northeast region of India. *J. Geol. Soc. India*, **62,** 680-695.

Bhattacharya, Pankaj M., Majumdar, R.K. and Kayal, J.R., 2002. Fractal dimension and b-value mapping in northeast India. *Curr. Sci.*, **82(12),** 1486-1491.

Bhattacharya, P.M., Pujol, J., Majumdar, R.K. and Kayal, J.R., 2005a. Relocation of earthquakes in the northeastern region using joint hypocentre determination method. *Curr. Sci.*, **89,** 1404-1413.

Bhattacharya, P.M., Mukhopadhyay, S., Majumdar, R.K. and Kayal, J.R., 2005b. Crustal velocity structure studies in the northeast India by joint hypocentre determination and simultaneous inversion. Proc. Seminar *East Crust*, Indian School of Mines, Dhanbad.

Bhattacharya, S.N., 1974. The crust-mantle structure of the Indian peninsula from surface wave dispersion. *Geophys. J.R. Astr. Soc.*, **36,** 273-283.

Bhattacharya, S.N., 1981. Observation and inversion of surface wave group velocities across central India. *Bull. Seismol. Soc. Am.*, **71,** 1489-1501.

Bhattacharya, S.N., 1992. Crustal and upper mantle velocity structure of India from surface wave dispersion. *Curr. Sci.*, **62,** 94-100.

Bhattacharya, S.N. and Dattatrayam, R.S., 2003. Some characteristics of recent earthquake sequences in peninsular India. *Gond. Geol. Magz.*, **5,** 67-85.

Bhattacharya, S.N. and Kayal, J.R., 2005. Seismicity of the Himachal Himalaya: Constraint from local seismic network. *Geol. Surv. India Sp. Pub.*, **85,** 71-79.

Bhattacharya, S.N., Prakash, C. and Srivastava, H.N., 1986. Microearthquake observations around Thein dam in northwest Himalayas. *Phys. Earth Planet. Inter.*, **44,** 169-178.

Bhattacharya, S.N., Ghosh, A.K., Suresh, G., Baidya, P.R. and Saxena, R.C., 1997. Source parameters of Jabalpur earthquake of May 22, 1997, *Curr. Sci.*, **73,** 855-863.

Bilek, S.L., 2007. Using earthquake rupture variations along the Sumatra-Andaman subduction system to examine fault zone variations. *Bull. Seism. Soc. Am.*, **97,** 502-570.

Bilham, R., 2001. Slow tilt reversal of the Lesser Himalaya between 1862 and 1992 at 78° E and bounds to the southeast rupture of the 1905 Kangra earthquake. *Geophys. J. Int.*, **144,** 1-23.

Bilham, R., 2005. A flying start, then a slow slip. *Science*, **308,** 1126-1127.

Bilham, R. and England, Phillip, 2001. Plateau 'pop up' in the great 1897 Assam earthquake. *Nature*, **410,** 806-809.

Bilham, R. and Hough, S.E., 2006. Future earthquakes on the Indian continent inevitable hazard, preventive risk. *South Asian J.*, **12,** 1-9.

Bilham, R., Blume Frederick, Bendick Rebecca and Gaur, V.K., 1998. Geodetic constraints on the Translation and deformation of India: Implications for future great Himalayan earthquakes. *Curr. Sci.*, **74,** 213-229.

Bilham, R., Gaur, V.K. and Molnar, P., 2001. Earthquakes: Himalayan seismic hazard. *Science*, **293,** 1442-1444.

Bilham, R., Engdahl, E.R., Feldl, N. and Satyabala, S.P., 2005. Partial and complete rupture of the Indo-Andaman plate boundary 1847-2004. *Seism. Res. Letts.*, **76,** 299-311.

Billings, M.P., 1954. *Structural Geology*. 2nd ed., Prentice Hall, New York, 514 p.

Billington, S., Isacks, B.L. and Barazangi, M., 1977. Spatial distribution and focal mechanisms of mantle earthquakes in the Hindu Kush-Pamir region: A contorted Benioff zone. *Geology*, **5,** 699-704.

Bird, P., 1978. Interaction of intra-continental subduction in the Himalaya. *J. Geophys. Res.*, **83,** 4975-4987.

Bird, P. and Toksöz, M.N., 1977. Strong attenuation of Rayleigh waves in Tibet. *Nature*, **266,** 161-163.

BIS, 2004. Seismic Zoning Map of India. Bureau Indian Standard publication, New Delhi, India.

Biswas, S.K., 1987. Regional tectonic framework, structure and evolution of the western marginal basins of India. *Tectonophysics*, **135,** 307-327.

Bisztricsany, E., 1958. A new method for determination of the magnitude of earthquakes. *Geofiz Kozlemen*, **7,** 69-96.

Bodin, P. and Horton, S., 2004. Source parameters and tectonic implications of aftershocks of the Mw 7.6 Bhuj earthquake of 26 January 2001. *Bull. Seism. Soc. Am.*, **94,** 818-827.

Bolt, B.A., 1999. *Earthquakes, A Primer*, 4th edition. W.H. Freeman NY, 366 p.

Borman, P., 1971. Location of teleseismic events by means of body-wave records at station Moxa (in German: Ortung teleseismischer Ereignisse aus Raumwellenregistrierungen der Station Moxa), *Monatberichte der ADW*, **13,** 10-12, 847-852.

Bott, M.H.P. and Dean, D.S., 1972. Stress systems at young continental margins. *Nature*, **235,** 23-25.

Bowin, C., 1973. Origin of the Ninety East Ridge from the studies near the equator. *J. Geophys. Res.*, **78,** 6029-6043.

Brown, L., Zhao, W., Nelson, K., Hauck, M., Alsdorf, D., Ross, A., Cogan, M., Clark, M., Liu, X. and Che, J., 1996. Bright spots, structure and magmatism in southern Tibet from INDEPTH seismic reflection profiling. *Science*, **274,** 1688-1690.

Brune, J.N., 1970. Tectonic stress and the spectra of seismic shear waves from earthquakes. *J. Geophys. Res.*, **75,** 4997-5009.

Brune, J.N., 1976. The physics of earthquake strong motion. *In:* Seismic Risk and Engineering Decisions, C. Lomnitz and E. Rosenblueth (eds.). Elsevier, Amsterdam, pp. 141-177.

Brune, J.N. and Allen, C., 1967. A microearthquake survey of the San Andreas fault system in southern California. *Bull. Seism. Soc. Am.*, **57,** 277-296.

Brune, J.N. and Singh, D.D., 1986. Continent-like crustal thickness beneath the Bay of Bengal sediments. *Bull. Seism. Soc. Am.*, **76,** 191-203.

Bullen, K.E., 1939. The crustal structure of New Zealand region as inferred from the study of seismic waves. Proc. 6th Pacific Sci. Cong., 103-110.

Bullen, K.E., 1965. *An introduction to the theory of seismology* (3rd ed.), Cambridge Univ. Press, London and New York.

Bullen, K.E. and Bolt, B.A., 1985. *An introduction to the theory of seismology* (4th ed.). Cambridge Univ. Press, U.K.

Burdick, L.J. and Langston, C.A., 1977. Modeling crustal structure through the use of the converted phases in teleseismic body waveforms. *Bull. Seismol. Soc. Am.*, **67,** 677-691.

Burke, K. and Dewey, J.F., 1973a. Plume-generated triple junctions: Key indicators in applying plate tectonics to old rocks. *J. Geophys. Res.*, **81,** 406-433.

Burke, K. and Dewey, J.F., 1973b. An outline of Precambrian plate movement. *In:* D.H. Tarling and S.K. Runcorn (eds.), Implications of Continental Drift to the Earth Sciences, v. 2, Academic Press, London, pp. 1035-1045.

Burke, K., Dewey, L.F., Edelstein, A., Kidd, W.S.F., Nelson, K.D., Sengor, A.M.C. and Stroup, J., 1978. Rift and sutures of the world (NASA-CR-175201) compiled for Goddard Space Flight Center, Greenbelt, Maryland. Albany Global Tectonics Group, State Univ. New York, Albany, NY, 238 p.

Burrard, S.G., 1915. Origin of the Indo-Gangetic trough, commonly called Himalayan foredeep. *Proc. Roy. Soc. Lond.*, **91A,** 220-238.

Burtman, V.S. and Molnar, P. 1993. Geological and geophysical evidence for deep subduction of continental crust beneath the Pamir. Tech. Rep Sp. Paper 281, Geol. Soc. Am.

Calhaem, I.M., Haines, A.J. and Lowry, M.A., 1977. An intermediate-depth earthquake in the central region of the South Island used to determine a local crustal thickness. *N. Z. J. Geol. Geophys.*, **20,** 353-361.

Catchings, R.D. and Kohler, W.M., 1996. Reflected seismic waves and their strong shaking during the 1989 Loma Prieta, California earthquake. *Bull. Seism. Soc. Am.*, **86,** 1401-1416.

Chadha, R.K., 1994. Estimation of T-waves in the Indian Ocean between Srilanka and Southern India. *Pure and Appl. Geophys.*, **142(2),** 319-328.

Chadha, R.K., 1995. Role of dykes in induced seismicity at Bhatsa reservoir, Maharashtra, India. *Pure and App. Geophys.*, **145,** 155-165.

Chadha, R.K., Gupta, H.K., Kumpel, H.J., Mandal, P., Nageswara Rao, A., Narendra Kumar, Radhakrishna, I., Rastogi, B.K., Raju, I.P., Sarma, C.S.P., Satyamurthy, C. and Satyanarayana, H.V.S., 1997. Delineation of active faults, nucleation process and pore pressure measurements at Koyna (India). *Pure and Appl Geophys.*, **150,** 551-562.

Chander, R., 1988. Interpretation of observed ground level changes due to the 1905 Kangla earthquake, northwest Himalaya. *Tectonophysics*, **149,** 289-298.

Chander, R., 1989. Southern limits of major earthquake ruptures along the Himalaya between 75° and 90° E. *Tectonophysics*, **170,** 115-123.

Chandra, U., 1975. Seismicity, earthquake mechanisms and tectonics of Burma, 20°N-28°N. *Geophys. J. Roy Astro. Soc.*, **40,** 367-381.

Chandra, U., 1977. Earthquakes of peninsular India – A seismotectonic study. *Bull. Seism. Soc. Am.*, **67,** 1387-1413.

Chandra, U., 1978. Seismicity, earthquake mechanisms and tectonics along the Himalayan mountain range and vicinity. *Phys. Earth Planet. Inter.*, **16,** 109-131.

Chandra, U., 1992. Seismotectonics of Himalaya. *Curr. Sc.*, **62,** 40-71.

Chandrasekaran, A.R., 1994. Evaluation of design earthquake parameters for a site and utilization of strong motion data. *Curr. Sci.*, **67,** 353-357.

Chandrasekaran, A.R. and Das, J.D., 1990. Strong motion arrays in India and characteristics of recent recorder events. *Bull. Ind. Soc. EQ. Tech.*, **27,** 1-66.

Chandrasekaran, A.R. and Das, J.D., 1992. Strong motion arrays in India and analysis of data from Shillong array. *Cur. Sci.*, **62,** 233-250.

Chandrasekaran, A.R. and Das, J.D., 1994. Analysis of strong motion accelerograms of northeast India earthquake of August 6, 1988. *Inst. Engg. Rep.*, **75,** 1-11.

Chandrasekhar, D.V. and Mishra, D.C., 2002. Some geodynamic aspects of Kutch basin and seismicity: An insight from gravity studies. *Curr. Sci.*, **83(4),** 492-498.

Chandrasekhar, D.V., Mishra, D.C., Singh, B., Vijayakumar, V. and Burgmann, R., 2004. Source parameters of the Bhuj earthquake, India of January 26, 2001 from height and gravity changes. *Geophys. Res. Lett.*, **31,** L 19608, doi: 10.1029/2004 GLO 20768.

Chang Ta, 1963. The geology of China. U.S. Deptt. of Commerce, Joint Publication Research Service, Washington DC., 548 p.

Chatelain, J.L., Roecker, S.W., Hatzfeld, D. and Molnar, P., 1980. Microearthquake seismicity and fault plane solutions in the Hindukush region and their tectonic implications. *J. Geophys. Res.*, **85,** 1365-1387.

Chatterjee, S.N. and Bhattacharya, S.N., 1992. Microearthquake surveys and seismicity in western Himalaya. *Geol. Soc. India Mem.*, **23,** 23-44.

Chaudhury, H.M. and Chatterjee, S.N., 1981. Microearthquake survey in the hot spring area in Parbati valley, Himachal Pradesh, India. *J. Volc. Geothermal Res.*, **9,** 29-30.

Chen, W.P. and Kao, H., 1996. Seismotectonics of Asia: Some recent progress. *In:* The Tectonic Evolution of Asia, A. Yin and M. Harrison (ed). Cambridge Univ. Press, New York, pp 37-62.

Chen, W.P. and Molnar, P., 1977. Seismic moments of major earthquakes and the average rate of slip in central Asia. *J. Geophys. Res.*, **82,** 2945-2969.

Chen, W.P. and Molnar, P., 1981. Constraints on the seismic wave velocity structure beneath the Tibetan plateau and their implications. *J. Geophys. Res.*, **86,** 5937-5962.